TEACHING FROM THE
MIDDLE OF THE ROOM

TEACHING FROM THE MIDDLE OF THE ROOM

Inviting Students to Learn

Frank Thoms

Stetson Press

Teaching from the Middle of the Room
Frank Thoms

Stetson Press
181 Market Street, Suite 14
Lowell, MA 01852

ISBN 978-0-615-35891-8

Library of Congress Control Number: 2010903078

Manufactured in the United States of America

To my mentors Delmar W. Goodwin, Barrie Rodgers, and David Mallery, each of whom cajoled, guided, and opened doors inside the beautiful world of the classroom.

BRIEF CONTENTS

CONTENTS

PART I   What Can We Do Immediately?

Teachers need specifics when they commit to make changes in their purpose and practice. Part I offers concrete strategies that build on what teachers know and do well.

PART II   How Can We Develop Our Teaching Practice?

When changing practices, teachers discover a need to reflect and consider broader perspectives. Part II takes a longer view of teaching, offers ideas to deepen practice, and addresses hard questions.

Part IV   What Can We Learn from Beyond the Culture of Schools?

If teachers commit to changing practice, taking radical steps above and beyond old methods will make a difference. Part IV explores ways to move beyond the norm.

Part V   How Do We Find Our Calling?

Ultimately, successful teaching requires understanding our purpose and ourselves. Part V invites teachers to explore their inner teacher and encourages them to transform when and if and when they feel the need.

Dan Hilliard had been teaching more than ten years. He was good at it; at least that's what his students told him. They liked his quirky qualities and sense of humor, especially his bad puns. His colleagues respected his ideas in the faculty room and at department meetings. His classroom was arranged much as he found it, desks in neat rows and columns facing his desk and a whiteboard.

He arrived early and left late every day, except Fridays. He prepared well-designed lessons to stimulate his students to question and think and to engage their curiosity. While he would not call himself a lecture-style teacher, he orchestrated discussions, rarely hesitating to jump in to offer elaborate explanations. His students enjoyed his involvement, and they rarely failed to pay attention. Time passed quickly in Mr. Hilliard's class.

He loved teaching, no doubt about it. He told everyone he looked forward to Mondays. Yet, he yearned for something more, something different. He had tried role-plays and simulations. Once, he and his students published a Soviet newspaper proclaiming the thoughts of Lenin and Stalin. He knew he was doing his best, but he sensed a longing to move beyond his comfort zone.

One day as he was taking attendance, he noticed that Sam, who sat in the middle of the middle row, was absent. Sam had never missed class. As he wondered, a streak of sunlight crossed Sam's desk. Slowly, Dan stepped forward, hesitated, and then moved towards Sam's seat. He sat down, remaining still and pensive. His students began to whisper to each other but soon became quiet. As he slowly looked around, he saw them looking at him—and at each other. He felt them behind him, as well. Occasionally, he had moved the desks into a horseshoe, but his students were used to seeing his face, and except for those sitting in the front row, saw only the backs of the heads of peers. Now they were looking at one another, wondering what their teacher was about to do. (He had surprised them before.) But Dan remained quiet and pensive.

After a few minutes, he asked a question. Later, when telling the story, he could not remember the question, but it was one that he asked to encourage discussion. After a long minute, Mary responded.

Instead of restating her idea and elaborating, Dan remained quiet. After another silence, Peter commented on Mary's point, which alerted several others. After a few minutes, Rebecca asked Mr. Hilliard for his thoughts. As he was about to launch forth, he hesitated. Then, he asked another question. The discussion resumed and soon broke up into small-group conversations.

Normally positioned in the front of the room, Dan usually would ask students to stop talking among themselves and pay attention. This time, he let the process play itself out. The room became noisier than usual, and somewhat chaotic—surely not a time for his principal to walk in.

He looked at the clock and saw there were about five minutes left. Normally, he would make his last one or two points; he often spoke beyond the bell hoping his students would remember his words. This time, he decided to give them time to absorb what they had been discussing, particularly since he did not know the content of the small-group conversations, except for those nearer to him.

He raised his hand to get his students' attention and asked them to take out a piece of paper and write:

1. a big idea they had discovered
2. how they plan to pursue their learning at home
3. a question they would like to focus on in class tomorrow

For the next few moments, he could have heard a pin drop.

As the bell rang, they stood up, put their responses in the outbox, then left. Dan remained in Sam's seat. "I think I'm on to something," he said to himself.

Dan's story illustrates the conundrum facing teachers. He is well respected and works hard, but, as true with many of his colleagues, he senses something is missing. Standing at the front of the room limits his options, but by sitting in Sam's seat, he discovers new possibilities. Dan made this decision on his own. Had he been told to make this move, he may well have resisted and held on to his own ways, ones he had practiced daily. Instead, he accepted the invitation of the empty desk. He had accepted invitations before, such as one from his colleague, Angela, to experiment with returning homework without grading to see if students would continue to do it. He and his colleagues were open to new ideas when they could choose to try them. But, when the administration insisted they use a new approach, they often feigned to use it while continuing with their own practices. Change, Dan understood, comes best from invitations, not from edicts.

A teacher myself, I wrote *Teaching from the Middle of the Room: Inviting Students to Learn* as an invitation for traditional, resistant teachers to embrace change. It is no secret that we are frustrated by a double-edged predicament: Reformers plead that we teach critical thinking skills, creativity, and effective communication to meet the challenges of a global world, and at the same time, school officials insist that we meet the tireless demands of annual state and federal testing. In addition, we face expanding curriculums, larger classes, and smaller budgets. It's no wonder we retreat into the cocoons of our classrooms, which remain the same private, isolated worlds of *our* childhood classrooms.

Our students, however, are different than we were at their age. The more time they spend alone watching TV, playing video games, text messaging, tweeting, and conversing on cell phones, the less time they have for thinking and learning—for spending time with their minds. They are becoming conduits of information without reflection—without ownership. The digital culture holds their attention by demanding immediate responses with hardly any concern for content;

not responding immediately means, "You're not my friend." There is anxiety here. Multitasking—as good as students may claim to be and as much as we may admire it—means to dart in and out of different media without taking ownership of any part. The mind can only attend to one cognitive task at a time.

As teachers we have an opportunity to make a significant impact right now if we choose. To start, we must relinquish control from the front of the room. Unless we are willing to let go of this delivery mode of teaching, we will not be able to meet today's students on their terms. They simply are not receptive to what we have to say, certainly not for the entire day. We need to meet them halfway—perhaps more than halfway—if we expect to become their teachers.

At the same time, we must not succumb to the electronic media blitz. If we do, we too will become conduits for the contents of others, of Big Brother, if you will. We will become clay in the hands of the media conglomerates, in conjunction with Disney's manipulation of princesses and faeries in the lives of little girls, and more recently, Disney XD, a brand aimed at boys from ages six to fourteen.

Already, we've lost the allegiance of children. We feel it every day, as we scramble to reel them in, to win their attention, to engage their minds. The more we ratchet up our traditional ways, the less connected they become. Reaching them, however, remains *the* challenge for us, more so than coping with state and federal testing or overloaded curriculums, which are also obstacles. Unless we diversify our teaching and focus on creating learning opportunities, we will simply teach to deaf ears. Children's brains are wired by their upbringing. Had they grown up learning to do chores, to postpone gratification, and to engage in free play, they would be better suited to learn as we did.

Few children have had opportunities to learn frustration tolerance because they get instant gratification from their electronic devices and from over-indulgent, anxiety-ridden, helicopter parents. Few children have free time with peers, as their lives are closely supervised and over-scheduled. Increasing numbers live in mixed-family households without extended family support. In 1996, Robert Evans alerted us to this situation:

[Students] are becoming steadily more disadvantaged and difficult to teach. This shift paints a portrait of social disintegration in America, a steady abandoning of direct care and support for the young by the other institutions on which our society and successful schooling have depended—most notably the family.[1]

Evans cites compelling evidence including:

- The nuclear family (two parents—one breadwinner, one homemaker—and two children) now constitutes only seven percent of all households (in 1950, it was sixty percent).

- Almost fifty percent of kindergartners can expect that their parents will divorce and that they will spend at least five years in a single parent home.

- Twenty-five percent of children currently live with only one parent (in 1960, fewer than ten percent did).

- Twenty-five percent of school-age children live below the poverty line.

- Thirty-one percent of births are to unmarried mothers (in 1950 it was five percent).[2]

And, Evans's research came before the coming of today's media-nurtured children, as Marc Prensky stridently identifies: "Our students have changed radically," he writes, "Today's students are no longer the people our educational system was designed to teach."[3] Given the overwhelming social upheavals that children face, combined with their digitally-wired brains, we have little choice but to respond to them in new and innovative ways.

This book confronts this crisis by encouraging educators to shift from delivering knowledge and skills to concentrating instead on what students learn in our classrooms every day. The intention of teaching is, after all, to cause learning. It's not what we *teach*—essential as it may seem—but what students *learn* that counts. When we make this shift, we step away from the front of the room to teach from the middle, alongside students to interact and connect with their learning; to enrich their thinking, creativity, and communication; and to assess their progress, make accommodations, and adjust to their needs as necessary.

Unless we commit to this shift, students will never learn how to teach themselves. Having an education ultimately means to learn *and* to know how to learn. We can be instrumental in this process only by making it possible for students to learn from us and with us. Students can be instrumental in this process only when their minds become engaged and committed to worthwhile pursuits. Otherwise, they are wasting their time in our classrooms.

As a lifelong teacher, I empathize with our profession's successful resistance to the reform efforts in the past century, as we have never been invited to participate as decision-makers or leaders. Instead, we feigned compliance when it was required, but then persisted to teach as our teachers had taught us, as evidenced by the continuing prevalence of whole-class lessons.

At the same time, some of us initiated changes at the classroom level but failed to make much headway. In the 1970s, for example, I participated in the open-education movement and implemented an exemplary open-education classroom, based on my teaching at a progressive primary school in Oxfordshire, England. Before the end of the decade, however, my efforts were reabsorbed into a traditional middle school. So much for change.

But the days of traditional teaching are numbered, as Marc Prensky indicated. In my work as a consultant during the past ten years with thousands of teachers in over one hundred twenty-five schools, I'm compelled to agree with Prensky. More and more teachers tell me students are less able to pay attention, when more likely they are paying attention to everything. Meanwhile, teachers feel like frustrated mail carriers with mailbags over-stuffed with the demands of the No Child Left Behind act (NCLB), rising state standards, local board mandates, and curriculums forcing them to teach more in less time. The faster they teach, the less they feel they deliver.

Educators face a unique challenge. Unlike previous generations, we now teach inside an unfamiliar culture, moving towards an unknown future; we cannot teach as we were taught if we intend to meet the demands of today's global world. As Einstein wisely intimated, "We can't solve problems by using the same kind of thinking we used when we created them."

Many teachers tell me they are waiting for leadership to undo what is no longer working. They also say they want to be invited to the table and not told what to do. In schools that support professional learning communities, they join administrators to reform teaching, sometimes taking the lead. But most still remain in isolated classrooms and need help but are afraid to ask for fear of being judged. Staying in their rooms, not causing a stir keeps them safe—and preserves their contracts.

Ironically, however, as teachers we are the deciders. We can change if we wish. We can stop doing what no longer works, start using better practices, and nurture what we already do well. We do not have to wait for leadership to guide us. We do not have to act out of fear. Except for those of us who are required to execute scripted lessons, we decide how we teach.

We need to find the courage to take creative steps to meet the needs of our students. We need to commit to make learning happen every day through effective lessons designed to deliver honest content, enduring understandings, relevant skills, and lifelong learning. We will then make the difference between an education geared towards the past and one headed for the future.

If we move beyond the embedded academic concentration in schools, we will enrich our teaching. Academic abilities—verbal and mathematical reasoning—are only two forms of intelligence that have value, but not to the exclusion of others. We must include all forms of intelligence at an equal level, especially creative and emotional intelligence, if we are to serve our students well. When we cut the arts to make more room to teach academics—often with "drill and kill" sessions to prepare for tests—we deprive children of the right and opportunity to discover and develop their gifts.[4]

The impetus for this book, which had been brewing for years, surfaced one October day when I observed fourteen ninth-grade teachers talking non-stop at their students. These were the same young, energetic teachers who, in a three-day workshop before the opening of school, expressed impatience with discussing interactive teaching techniques. They wanted, instead, to set up their small learning communities in preparation for their first days and weeks. So we decided to give over the third workshop day for this purpose. I cautioned them to remember that the most important ingredient in their success would be the quality of their teaching in their classrooms. Fortunately, my contract included returning to the school to coach and to provide workshops throughout the year.

I was eager, then, to return to observe them in their respective classrooms, particularly to see how they designed lessons, engaged students, formed relationships, and activated thinking. The coordinators of the program decided not to tell them when I was coming.

I was unprepared for what I saw. I observed students in each classroom sitting passively at desks in rows, listening or whispering to one another. Except for occasional responses to the first hand raised, no interactions happened between teacher and students or among students. Not one. By the end of the day, I imagined them as seated, bronzed figures traveling from class to class. The next day, I composed a six-page letter to the teachers, which became the foundation for this book.

Several teachers told me later that they wished they had known I was coming so they could have prepared better. After all, the idea of delivering a dog-and-pony show when it counts resides deeply in the profession. We all remember days when our own teachers were observed. Often, we played along to help them impress visitors.

This book is structured to meet the needs of readers that include teachers, professors, administrators, and others interested in what happens in classrooms. Each chapter concludes with a "Reflection" in which Dan Hilliard and his colleagues offer their insights. This is followed by "Points to Pursue" to inspire readers' further thinking and discussion. Each chapter stands alone, so readers can select those that interest them.

For example, those who want to re-examine lecturing or talking from the front of the room might begin with Chapter 1, "Implement 10-2 Thinking." Those wishing to explore larger issues facing teachers might begin with Chapter 7, "See the Big Picture." Or, to consider the cosmological perspective as it applies to the classroom, read Chapter 19, "Invoke the Cosmos."

As with chapters, each part of the book stands alone, again inviting readers to find their entry point:

- **Part I.** To learn about specific, doable strategies, begin by reading Part I, "What Can We Do Immediately?" and learn how to modify and extend common teaching skills to make them work from the middle of the room.

- **Part II.** To take a longer view, begin at Part II, "How Can We Develop Our Teaching Practice?" and discover the strength of seeking wisdom both old and new, and ponder difficult questions facing classroom teachers.

- **Part III.** To consider obstacles impeding effective teaching, begin at Part III, "What Must We Change?" and learn not only about failing traditional practices but also about sensible and practical alternatives.

- **Part IV.** To explore more radical ideas and perspectives, begin at Part IV, "What Can We Learn from Beyond the Culture of Schools?" and examine out-of-the-box points of view to freshen and enlighten teaching and learning.

- **Part V.** To seek knowing the inner teacher, begin at Part V, "How Do We Find Our Calling?" and discover the significance of teaching as a personal and collective calling, which requires a never-ending search for meaning and a willingness to transform—essential qualities for becoming a complete teacher.

In addition, teachers and professors in particular are encouraged to examine the "Teaching Manifesto" in the Appendix before and/or after reading the book. The Teaching Manifesto provides guidelines for teaching from the middle of the room, and invites teachers to sign and date their commitments to follow its principles. Other interested readers might want to read it to gain perspective on what's possible when teachers choose to make learning happen in the classroom.

Ultimately, *Teaching from the Middle of the Room: Inviting Students to Learn* serves as a friend, companion, and mentor for creating learning in the classroom, as it nurtures true collegiality, through which the whole becomes greater than the sum of its parts. Teachers at all levels who read this book—especially with colleagues—will become better teachers. Administrators, parents, board members, and interested citizens who read it will be better able to help teachers make the necessary shift to teach from the middle of the room. Ultimately, everybody has a vested interest in education—and in this book.

What Can We Do Immediately?

As teachers, we develop extraordinary skills. We instruct, organize, analyze, synthesize, create, articulate, observe, evaluate, write, initiate, study, plan, communicate, persuade, motivate, process, prioritize, problem-solve, meet deadlines, use technologies, negotiate, relate, listen, remember, reflect, adapt, diagnose, advise, counsel, coach, empathize, follow through, and so on. We call on any and all of these skills throughout the day. It is common knowledge that in the number of mental tasks we need to perform in a given day—up to three thousand—we are second only to air traffic controllers. We keep an eye on the big picture and pay attention to minute details at the same time. And, we do it alone.

No wonder, then, we balk when told to drop what we are doing (and may be doing well) to change to a new approach, new curriculum, or new method. The act of being told what to do signals that we are inadequate and builds resentment within us. Hence, the basic premise of this book rests on respect for the hard work we as teachers do every day, and invites us to reconsider our current practices in light of the needs and demands of today's students, culture, and global world.

Part I asks us to build on what we already do well by reframing, restructuring, and reorienting common practices in new directions to improve learning in the classroom. This shift will have an enormous effect on the motivation, involvement, and success of our students and will deepen our satisfaction with the important work we do every day.

Each chapter in Part I offers accessible and proven ways to teach from the middle of the room. These methods represent a small sample of what we can do immediately to teach successfully in today's rapidly changing world.

CHAPTER 1

Implement 10-2 Thinking

"Dennis . . . Peter . . . Mary . . . Sebastian . . . José . . . OK, all here except Miranda and Natasha.

"A reminder: Tomorrow I will review this week's material for the test you will take on Friday. Be sure to go over your notes and reread Chapter 12 in your textbook."

"Which chapter, Ms. Bernardi?"

"Chapter 12, Ellie.

"Now for today's lecture. We will continue discussing Lincoln's presidency prior to the outbreak of the Civil War. Yesterday, we spoke about the Lincoln-Douglas debates. Today, I will begin explaining the results of those seven debates. Please take out your notebooks and begin by copying down the quotations I've put on the board . . . "

We've all been here. As students, we quickly learn the routines of the classroom. The longer we're in school the more consistent they became. When we become teachers, we continue the pattern. Taking attendance, collecting homework, setting the lesson, delivering material, winding down, assigning homework, dismissing . . . We know the drill.

"Do your teachers talk most of the time?" I ask students whenever I have the chance. "Yes," I hear over and over. Even from my grandchildren. I wouldn't worry if these responses were atypical, but unfortunately they reflect the research in schools across the country. As a consultant for the past ten years, I have been hoping to see a shift in this pattern, but I rarely have found it.

What keeps Allegra Bernardi lecturing in her American History class day after day? She did it in her first years most likely because she was nervous about letting her students take over with their questions and comments. She figured if she kept talking, she would maintain better control. She would probably argue now that she needs to meet the pressures of the No Child Left Behind act (NCLB) and state assessments, so covering as much material as possible is essential. She might add, as well, that this is the way teachers have always taught. Besides, her students are used to this approach, and parents also expect it, as it is the approach with which they grew up. And, some of Allegra's colleagues have told her they might lose their jobs if they deviate from this embedded norm, since it is "the way teachers teach."

But, do we realize the impact of all this talking? Are we aware of what's happening in our students' minds when we deliver information day after day? What if we stepped back for a moment to visualize them sitting at desks taking notes from us for a period, then doing the same in three other classes every day? Four classes a day, one hundred eighty minutes, about five hundred hours in a year. Or, what about elementary children who sit at their desks listening to multiple series of instructions throughout the day, followed by seatwork with workbooks and repetitive worksheets? What's happening in their minds? How are they processing? What values are they internalizing? What are they actually learning?

Unfortunately, we rarely take time to find out. Yet, we complain that more and more students do not relate to our lectures and whole-class lessons, are not willing to do homework, and do not care about quizzes and tests. We sometimes feel as if we are talking to strangers.

Yet, most of us persist. What, then, will jolt us to stop talking so much? What will convince us to reframe our teaching to teach from the middle of the room?

- We could begin by visualizing ourselves sitting at a student's desk (like Dan Hilliard) and activating and engaging students' minds instead of having them face us and take notes.

- We could recall those teachers who deferred from talking to the whole class, and instead, invited us to respond to provocative questions, creative ideas, and rigorous projects.

- We could acknowledge that copying notes or filling out worksheets has little or no relevance to digitally-wired children.

- We could recognize that the ultimatums of global connectivity and complexity require that we become active agents in creating and designing our place in the world. Passive learning sends the wrong message.

Evidence is building in research, journals, and literature for developing and implementing active and engaging teaching. One example, the Partnership for 21st Century Skills, a leading coalition of teachers, industry, library groups, educational providers, and government groups, advocates the following skills that adults will need to succeed in the decades ahead:[5]

- Information and communication skills, including media literacy
- Thinking and problem-solving skills, including: critical thinking; systems thinking; problem identification, formulation, and solution; creativity and intellectual curiosity
- Interpersonal and self-direction skills: collaboration, self-direction, accountability, adaptability, and social responsibility
- Global awareness
- Financial, economic, and business literacy; entrepreneurial skills to enhance workplace productivity and career options
- Civic literacy

None of these skills can be learned from sitting and listening. Yet, we continue to make students listen to us as *the* primary way to learn in our classrooms. Instead, we might heed the words of the Spanish proverb, "What one does, one becomes" or the wisdom of the Buddha, "We are what we practice." If students "practice" sitting at desks half-listening to us, what will they "become"? How well will they know themselves? What will they care about? What skills will they have to prosper in the twenty-first century?

So, where do we begin?

We need, first, to recognize and honor our deep commitment to students, without which we would not be teaching. We work hard and care for each and every one of them, and often leave school exhausted. We know—as the research has confirmed—we are the most important factor for their success in our classrooms. How, then, can we use our caring and commitment to turn our talking as delivery into talking for learning?

We can begin by asking ourselves: "How can I take advantage of my conversational skills and turn away from delivery of information and knowledge and move towards making learning happen *in my classroom* every day?"

We can visualize letting go of repetitive, whole-group talking, and instead, imagine using words as brain stimulators, as work energizers, and as learning motivators. We can pay more attention to students' ideas rather than insisting they listen and repeat what we say. We can activate ways to think, create, and design rather than to copy, memorize, and regurgitate, thus gaining confidence as we see students learning. We can say less and teach more. We can listen and learn about their learning—and learn from them.

Once we begin this process, we taste a new future. We gain a deeper satisfaction as more students retain what we teach. We relish seeing them active and involved. Suddenly, there is no turning back. We're no longer stuck in past practice, in which we relegated ourselves to the trash heap of talking teachers.

If we are to make this essential shift, we need tools. One of the best and most accessible is the principle of 10-2, which was developed over twenty-five years ago by Mary Budd Rowe.[6] It is a natural pathway for using our talking skills to stimulate student interest and learning based on a simple principle: For every ten minutes we provide information, knowledge, or skills, we give students two minutes to process.

Here are some examples of implementing and assessing the principle of 10-2:

- In math, after introducing improper fractions for about ten minutes, we ask students to work alone or in pairs or in groups for two minutes to create problems using these fractions.

- In history, after teaching an aspect of slavery as a cause of the Civil War for ten minutes or so, we can ask students to take two minutes to create a graphic organizer to demonstrate their understanding.

- In Language Arts, we can ask students not to write while giving a mini-lecture on the complexities of a Shakespear-

ean plot, and then ask them to write down what they heard/
learned.

- As students process during the two minutes, we can walk
  around and listen and adopt what we hear for our next ten-
  minute segment; when we talk or lecture nonstop, however,
  we do not learn what students are absorbing or not absorbing.

- After our final ten minutes, Rowe says to allow students five
  minutes to ask questions about the lesson. First, it provides
  them an opportunity to review their understandings of the
  lesson, and second, it provides us feedback about what they
  learned to indicate where we might take the next lesson.

- Instead of students taking notes continuously, the opportunity to process intermittently enables them to leave class
  retaining more—much more—than if we had talked the
  whole period.

- We can then assign homework directly related to what they
  have been learning and need to learn. This is home-practice
  that makes sense.

Implementing 10-2 Thinking, as I prefer to call it, is particularly
important for those of us who lecture. This age-old format usually
requires students to take notes throughout the period as we talk and
occasionally respond to questions. But, when we commit to 10-2
Thinking, we reshape our lectures into segments and plan for the two-
minute activities. At first, we and our students will find it challenging,
but we will persist when we see the benefits for our students and us.
Our classes will become more interesting.

The most significant value of 10-2 Thinking is that it allows us
to concentrate on student learning. It also enables students to participate in a way that mirrors their interactive lives (albeit mostly
through technology) outside of school. When we simply lecture, we
do not know until the test (way too late!) whether or not we are causing learning. When we use 10-2 Thinking, on the other hand, each
processing segment provides us (and students) immediate feedback
about to what is understood. Any time we teach and students are

"not there" we are wasting our time—and theirs. In the words of Dylan Wiliam:

> If students left the classroom before teachers have made adjustments to their teaching on the basis of what they have learned about the students' achievement, then they are already playing catch-up. If teachers do not make adjustments before students come back the next day, it is probably too late.[7]

These are profound words worth rereading.

The principle of 10-2 Thinking also applies to those of us who do not lecture but talk in lengthy segments, including we who teach at the elementary level. When introducing a unit of study, for example, we often speak at some length. It behooves us, then, to break up instructions into segments in which students can process and ask questions. And, we should intersperse our talking with questions to assess their thinking and understanding. When elementary teachers say they don't need to use the 10-2 Thinking principle, I share the story of Sheila Webb, a kindergarten teacher, who uses it consistently. "I love it!" she told me, "The students benefit so much from working with each other. The conversations are appropriate and relative to the lesson. Oftentimes, the reluctant students are right in the group instructions, talking about their own experiences or interpretations."

Another concern about allowing time for students to converse among themselves is the potential for gossip. On the contrary, the two minutes lets us listen in as they talk rather than surmising their thinking while we are talking extensively or lecturing. Besides, students welcome opportunities to talk with their peers and not have to sit quietly all period—and they appreciate having input in their own learning.

A side benefit, perhaps as important, of interactive processing time is that students and teachers must speak face-to-face, a skill sorely lacking in many digitally-savvy students. Speaking while looking into the eyes of one another brings a different dimension to learning, one that does not occur when students face teachers from desks in rows, or whenever they chat, tweet, text, or use cell phones.

When we lecture, we act as conduits, but when we choose 10-2 Thinking, we invoke the interactivity of language, the power of dialogue. We slow down and can apply "wait time" (another of Mary Budd Rowe's ideas) after asking a question to allow students to think before speaking. More than thirty years ago, Rowe advocated that teachers wait for three seconds before calling on students, instead of the 0.5 seconds that most did (and still do, I might add). By waiting three seconds, we invite students who usually hesitate to participate, encourage full sentences rather than one or two words, invite higher-order thinking, and make it more likely for students to respond and comment on each other's answers.[8] We can also wait another four-to-five seconds before we respond or move the question on—an idea suggested by Laura Reasoner Jones.[9] No more quick responses to quick questions. Instead, we invite deeper thinking to seek deeper answers, sometimes assigning one-minute writing intervals to search for clarifications and understandings. We begin to create a community of learners rather than act as a knowledge-dispensary center.

Many who lecture, however, argue that since some students do well, they believe lectures should work for the rest if only those students would put in more effort. But, this method reaches fewer and fewer of today's digitally-wired students. And those with learning disabilities, such as ADD, ADHD, and autism, struggle when listening and taking notes at the same time. In years past, many of these students would have been considered less smart and steered into the workforce. Now we know they deserve every opportunity to succeed.

Yet some of us still hesitate to cross this threshold to implement 10-2 Thinking for fear it will take time away from covering material. In a forty-five minute lecture, 10-2 "costs" about ten minutes. The obvious contradiction in this argument, however, grants that straight lecturing may allow more time for coverage but sacrifices opportunities for learning.

When we decide to commit to 10-2 Thinking, we do not need to be wedded to its framework; we might prefer, for example, 7-3, 15-3, and so on, depending on our students, the context of the material, and our purpose. Using this approach reminds us that the best learning occurs while we are teaching and not afterwards. Eventually, classrooms move towards greater processing times in relation to input. When learning becomes central, the ratio, for example, can shift from 10-2 to 2-10, where the dominant time focuses on processing serious content. Given the abundance of resources at students' fingertips, teachers can encourage students to seek information on their own at home, as Dan Hilliard did, and then apply their learning in class.

Once teachers realize the value and importance of creating engaged class time by concentrating on face-to-face conversations, they will take time to teach students how to pursue learning before class. When students understand the joy of coming to class to share and discuss what matters to them with their peers and teacher, they will become more willing to commit to exploring ideas on their own. Then, homework—home practice—can become a welcome precursor to attending class rather than a boring chore afterwards. Teachers can put a PowerPoint presentation online as a lecture to study before class. Such an approach appeals to students' desire to learn using electronic devices while in pursuit of worthwhile knowledge and understandings. Using thumbs to discover rather than to socialize is a novel idea indeed! Coming to class expecting to engage in conversation is so different from sitting and listening to the teacher!

Invoking conversation changes relationships. In the words of Margaret Wheatley,

> We acknowledge one another as equals.
> We try to stay curious about each other.
> We recognize that we need each other's help to become better listeners.
> We slow down so we have time to think and reflect.
> We remember that conversation is the natural way we humans think together.
> We expect it to be messy at times.[10]

Some of the greatest joys in my teaching included sitting in a circle with eighth graders and pondering each student's comment without squeezing it into the script of the lesson; asking "What do you mean?" or "What do others think?" rather than correcting and reinterpreting; deciding not to call on the first hand raised; waiting patiently for responses from reluctant speakers; taking time to reflect; putting students' insights on the board . . . How different this is from teaching as delivery. How special. How important.

So, we need to ask ourselves:

What do students take from interactive conversations?
What will we have taught?
What will they learn?
What will they remember later on?
How will they survive the pressures of testing while learning in such a slow curriculum?

The research makes clear that depth is more important for learning than breadth. Delving into material opens learning potential more than rushing through it. Teaching for understanding enables the mind to think intelligently when confronting new concepts and information, whereas teaching for rote memory disconnects learning and stymies long-term retention. By invoking 10-2 Thinking, we choose to step out from under the explanation umbrella and decide to engage in conversation. As we teach for understanding, we talk less, our students learn more—and so do we.

> *The bell is about to ring. Ms. Bernardi, appealing for her students to listen one last time, quickly summarizes her last point. As the bell rings, she points to the assignment on the board and asks them to be sure they've written it down. By then, half of her students have left their seats and are heading for the door . . .*

REFLECTION

Dan Hilliard and Allegra Bernardi have often discussed the impact of lecturing on learning. "Why do we do it," they wondered, "when we were often bored listening to lectures?" Dan has begun to move away from being the prime talker in his classroom. He likes 10-2 Thinking, as it improves chances for his students to learn. He struggled with it at first but soon found it workable—and satisfying. In fact, he realized that 10-2 Thinking has changed his perspective on teaching. Instead of thinking of teaching as providing information, he now sees it including frequent assessments to assure his students are learning. Checking in and listening to them has become essential to his teaching.

"If every teacher who lectured or talked a lot decided to use 10-2 Thinking," Dan thought to himself, "what a difference it would make throughout the school! Every student would leave every class having worked with the material taught—and would go home with something with which to practice!"

On the day Sam was absent, when Dan asked his students how they planned to pursue their learning at home, he realized he had shifted his conception of homework as well. He said to himself, "Why shouldn't they have more input about what to learn at home?"

He decided to ask Allegra to observe him because he not only wanted to show her how he was using 10-2 Thinking but also wanted her feedback. "What if," Dan said to her, "we made a pact to listen more and talk less to our students—and to let them give more input about their learning? What if our classrooms eventually became more like 2-10 Thinking!?"

"I think this is a good idea," Allegra said. "But we must be careful not to become stuck in either-or thinking. Sometimes, as you well know, we can talk to students for as long as twenty minutes and have their full attention. These times, what I call engaged talking, sometimes happen by surprise, when students are eager to take in what we have to say. It's like they're hungry for our words and hang on to every one. I do not want to give up those times."

"Neither do I," Dan replied.

POINTS TO PURSUE

☑   Give yourself a prescribed amount of time to talk on a topic and set a timer. Tell your students why you are doing this—and that they will need to participate more than they are used to. Using a timer makes for more efficient teaching. Make a video if you can.

☑   Try 10-2 Thinking, not once but for several weeks. Take time to introduce it and teach the process. Be patient with your students and yourself. Be flexible setting the proportions between input and process. Pay attention to their reactions. It will be worth it.

☑   Try using wait time for several weeks to see if the quality of student participation improves. Also, extend the time you respond to students as Laura Reasoner Jones suggests. Be patient, as this process takes time to work.

☑ If you have found successful ways to reduce your talking to increase time for learning, make a point to share it—or teach it—to a colleague. If you know of a colleague who has reduced the amount of talking in her teaching, observe to learn about what she is doing.

☑ Adopt Margaret Wheatley's principles and begin to build a conversation culture in your classroom, as messy as it might be. Let respect for your students be your guide.

☑ Pay attention to those moments when engaged talking works. What are the characteristics of such times? How much do students actually learn?

☑ Pay attention to the homework you give. Develop ways to encourage students to choose their homework and assess its effects on learning. Send a PowerPoint presentation home and see what happens the next day.

CHAPTER 2

Teach Literacy

"Okay class, for tonight I want you to begin our study of organelles by reading sections 1 and 2 of chapter 15 in the textbook, and answer the first five questions at the end. I will collect them before class. See you tomorrow."

We teach children to read during their first years in school, and by the time they reach middle school, we assume they know how. On the surface, this appears true for most children. But if we also assume they are able to read for meaning and understanding, we may need to think again. Comprehending textbooks, for example, is a challenge for many of our students, including how to answer questions at the end of chapters. Most students attempt to read the text first and then try to answer the assigned questions. Others decide to turn immediately to the questions then look for the answers in the text. Some struggle with other ways, hoping they will get it right. And others simply give up.

If we expect students to dissect and comprehend a textbook (or any book we use for that matter), then we cannot simply assign pages; we need to teach students how to read them. In fact, as English Language Arts teachers know well, all of us need to teach students how to read books in our field. In particular, we know how difficult textbooks are to read, as most are constructed as a series of "mention sentences"; that is, a series of disconnected sentences, each "correct" but not well connected and coherent. I learned this concept from Jim Grant, founder of Staff Development for Educators, at a workshop in 2004. He based his conclusions on close analysis of textbooks, and he attributes their "cleaned-up" quality to the textbook review committee of Texas.[11]

As a teacher, I only used textbooks when it was required. I found them challenging, and I often relied on my best memorizers during class to help me remember what I had assigned! I imagine that today's digitally-oriented students find them linear, cumbersome, and dull.

If we use textbooks, or any text materials, we need to do the following to assure that students learn:

1. We agree, first, to commit as much time as necessary to teach them how to be students of the text. Before we begin, we make sure the class understands not only our intent to teach the process of effective reading but also to learn the content.

2. We approach the text using a jigsaw, assigning different sections of a chapter to separate groups of students. We start by having students read their section closely, using Post-its or flags (if they know how) and taking brief notes in response to specific questions we pose. If the reading level is too challenging for some, we pair students and/or work with them directly, as we want everyone to be able to participate in the jigsaw.

3. Then, we group those who read the same section to meet and discuss their findings. Once they agree on answers to the questions, we have them write a common statement indicating their understanding. They also should generate further questions to stretch their thinking. We quickly check their common statements before they share to be sure they understand their section.

4. We then put one student (or pairs of students) from each group into mixed groups to report their findings. Having the common written statement and questions will assure consistency and help them focus on what they need to share.

5. Once the sharing is completed, each group can then approach selected questions at the end of the chapter (or questions we pose) and answer them together. Then, they can take time to reflect and summarize their understandings, perhaps using a graphic organizer. Finally, they might identify further questions to raise their curiosity about the implications of what they've learned.

6. We may want to repeat this practice (or variations) until we see that students understand how to read and learn from the text.

7. As reinforcement, we can assign part of a jigsaw in class and assign another part for home practice. Encourage them to use instant messaging to help each other, if necessary. We can join them if we'd like.

The net result of this in-class effort not only teaches students how to approach reading texts but also supports their efforts. It also lets them know that we recognize the challenge of becoming fluent in reading and writing—and that we will be there for them. We can be confident that when we assign future readings, their newfound literacy skills will give them a better chance for success. But if we fail to take this time, much of what we teach will not stick.

As an example, I observed teacher Ron Schultz lecture his sixth-grade students about the nature of history. He stood in front of the room, gave notes, and asked and answered questions. He appeared well prepared and was enjoying his students—and they were enjoying him. For homework, he assigned a one-page worksheet describing Sherlock Holmes as a detective. The students were expected to locate and highlight passages about Sherlock Holmes's skills and relate them to the tools of historians.

When I spoke with Ron about this particular homework assignment, he immediately indicated that it was way over their heads. I asked, then, why he gave it to them. After some conversation, he realized this assignment would have been better taught in class, because it not only would have engaged his students in the historical process (the Sherlock Holmes connection), but, more importantly, he would have been able to work alongside them.

His students might have addressed this task in a myriad of ways. They could have worked in pairs or in groups to connect the relationship between Holmes's tools as a detective with those of historians. They could have determined their own conclusions and shared them with the whole class in an attempt to reach consensus. They could have used their cell phones to text message one another or to seek the advice and opinion of people beyond the classroom. Questions to seek understandings and higher-order thinking undoubtedly would have arisen. It might well have turned into one of those magical hub-bub classes, full of energy, focused noise, and engagement, rather than one characterized by the restless behavior that often occurs during lecture-style teaching.

To continue with this Sherlock-Holmes example, what if Ron had asked students to create a play, casting detectives as historians? Or asked them to make pamphlets or thought-provoking posters? Or asked them to create a Holmes-Historian journal? They could have drafted a letter to convince their textbook publisher to include Holmes in the section, "What is History?" In the end, he could have asked them to write reflective essays and taken time to help them edit and rewrite in class. Eventually, the essays would make a class book, "What is an Historian?"

Or, he might have invited them to create public service announcements (PSAs) to persuade a younger audience to regard historians as detectives. The level of technology used to produce the PSA would depend on the sophistication of the students, and might include Microsoft Word, PowerPoint, iMovie and Movie Maker, and digital still camera or digital video camera. How exciting for them to use "their media" rather than exclusively paper and pencil!

This example ultimately demonstrates how Ron could have actively engaged students in learning *in the classroom*—and the endless possibilities available in the process. If, on the other hand, we teach assuming that students have all the tools necessary for learning, we miss opportunities for developing all-important literacy skills, a necessary prerequisite for success in the future. And, we miss engaging their minds.

REFLECTION

We need to become vigilant about the literacy levels of students. We can never assume they know how to read, write, and argue well, at any grade level. While they may appear able to read proficiently, they may be sliding along, concealing that they are less able. Dan Hilliard learned recently from a former good student from his first year of teaching that she "really learned to read" from his veteran colleague, Mel Goodwin, in her senior American Studies class.

Because we cannot make assumptions about what skills students possess, we need to provide opportunities for them to demonstrate their proficiencies. We also need to realize that once we've introduced a literacy skill, we need to reinforce it throughout the year. In fact, we need to teach traditional literacy *and* 21st century skills every day.[12] Dan has become aware of this imperative and spends increasing amounts of time putting both sets of skills at the center of his teaching.

POINTS TO PURSUE

☑ As a pre-assessment of reading and writing skills, pass out a short, provocative reading relevant to your subject or grade-level. Ask students to learn it and observe how they approach it. Do they simply read it? Do they use highlighters? Underline? Write in the margin? Ask clarifying questions? From this pre-assessment, you can determine where your students are and what skills you need to teach.

☑ Then, introduce another one-page reading. This time, teach students ways to approach the reading using focus questions, underlining, highlighting, etc. Also, allow time for them to use "think-pair-share," where students take time to reflect alone, then discuss their ideas with a partner (or two partners if you prefer), and then share with the whole class. Follow-up by soliciting their input about what works, then give a brief quiz the next day to assess their learning.

☑ As a class, take time to have a metacognitive discussion, to talk about students' thinking, their thinking about their thinking, and their awareness of how they think and use strategies, in comparing the results of these two exercises. Discuss the importance of comprehension, as well as generating authentic questions.

☑ If you are expected to use a textbook, particularly in the humanities, make every effort to incorporate additional narrative and interesting material whenever possible, since textbooks can be challenging for most students—and for some teachers. Make sure that questions are central to class discussions, particularly essential questions that provoke and stimulate evidentiary thinking.

☑ One way to stimulate learning and help students retain text materials is to ask students provocative questions before reading, or ask the end-of-the chapter questions. Such practice ups the ante in students' minds.[13]

☑ Do you know how your colleagues teach both literacy and 21st century skills? Find out, and then observe those who claim they do. You will learn from each another.

☑ What are you doing to teach 21st century skills? How can you justify that teaching these skills will not water down the academic curriculum? How can you convince others that teaching these skills is every bit as important as—perhaps more important than—academic skills? These are vital questions.

CHAPTER 3

Instill Skills

During workshops, I sometimes recount incidences of students who highlight whole paragraphs and even whole pages! Invariably, teachers chuckle.

We can remember as pupils how we fended for ourselves learning how to do school. We often had to figure out how to do homework, study for tests, take notes, write papers, complete projects, and organize. Those among us who did these things well often turned out to be the good students, while the rest of us coped as best we could.

When we think about it, parents and pupils share a surprising similarity: They learn how to do what they have to do on their own. We expect preparation for parenting to be uneven, as we have no parent-instruction institutions. But schools are institutions with a defined structure, run by teachers and support staff who guide students for thirteen years or longer. Yet, results belie our effectiveness.

Some among us, however, take time to teach students how to do school. I was fortunate to co-teach in my first years with a master teacher, Del Goodwin, who spent an extraordinary amount of time teaching students how to approach schoolwork, including how to take effective lecture notes, write essays, and prepare research papers (his "A Manual for the Writing of Research Papers,"[14] was exemplary). In those pre-rubric, pre-formative-assessment days, we spent an inordinate amount of time defining procedures and providing feedback to students.

The clarion calls for developing better assessment practices, implementing backwards design that brings focus to lessons and units,[15] and preparing for state and federal tests have encouraged teachers to focus on teaching skills to help students learn how to do school. While many disagree about the virtue of teaching to the test, at least teachers are paying attention to test-taking skills. But, as the research affirms, basic skills, especially literacy and 21st century skills, are neglected.[16]

In fact, teaching how to do school is largely ignored, as the chuckle from teachers at the opening of this chapter indicates. As students move through school, we assume they learn basic skills and procedures from their teachers in earlier years. Since almost everyone assigns homework, we believe students know how to do it. When we ask them to read a chapter, we assume they know how. After all, they've have had years of reading already. And when we say, "Take out your notebook," we take it for granted they know how to take notes. Besides, because we have so much content to cover, we feel we need to teach it as quickly as possible.

If we took time to interview students about their skills, we'd be astonished at their differing competency levels. When they fail at homework, for example, we often attribute it to lack of effort or unwillingness to try when, in fact, they may not have a clue as to what we want. When they take poor notes, we wonder about their motivation. Few students willingly speak out in class to ask for help for fear of appearing incompetent. And, when we see them highlight whole paragraphs and pages, we too chuckle.

Like most teachers, I watched as highlighters appeared in my students' pencil cases but paid them little attention, as they were ancillary to my teaching. I never imagined I should teach my students how to use them, even as I saw them highlight whole paragraphs and pages. I realize now I missed a perfect opportunity to incorporate a new tool to teach essential skills. I hope I can make up for my shortcomings in these pages.

Today, I would begin each year assuming my students do not have the skills needed in my classroom. When assigning homework, for example I would take time to be sure they understood my expectations and had the necessary tools. Before asking them to use highlighters as a learning tool (at the upper elementary, middle and high-school levels), I would do the following:

1. Find a provocative one-page piece of writing that will hook students into reading it.
2. Give each student two highlighters, each one a different color, for example one yellow and one blue.
3. Put a question on the board and ask them to use the yellow highlighter to search for information to support their think-

ing. Tell them to highlight words or phrases and not sentences or paragraphs.

4. Have the students take two minutes to compare their highlighting with a partner in preparation for a class conversation.

5. With the whole class, seek consensus about what should have been highlighted, then have students write out their thoughts and further questions they may have.

6. Put a second question on the board and ask them to use the blue highlighter to underline words and phrases in the same article. If they highlight the same words as they did with yellow, the words will appear green, which can stimulate further conversation.[17]

7. Again have them compare their highlighting with a peer and hold a class discussion, and have them write out their thoughts and conclusions.

8. An option at this point is to have students meet in groups to write a common statement in response to one or both of the questions.

9. Finally, hold a whole-class discussion to flesh out further questions and assess understandings.

When we focus our intention on using highlighters, we have the opportunity to put ourselves in our students' shoes, as we not only demonstrate how to highlight but also sit alongside them and provide feedback. Were we, instead, to lecture for a period and then give them a homework assignment to highlight, we would likely see colored paragraphs and pages the next day—or no highlighting at all.

Another approach that uses two highlighters in a one-page exercise is to have students use one color to mark what they think is significant and the other for what they find confusing. Again, the focus is on teaching how to use highlighters as tools for learning and retaining knowledge and understanding.

We provide a new and effective tool for practicing literacy skills—and, with persistence, we open new horizons—by putting students to work using highlighters in the classroom. This is a golden opportunity to develop and reinforce essential literacy skills, by activating the power of close, purposeful reading and rereading; by demonstrating the value of writing and rewriting to improve thinking; and by providing opportunities to discuss and argue concepts using evidence.

We can create similar exercises by introducing Post-it notes and flags: Ask students to search through a textbook (which they are usually not allowed to mark) and flag answers to questions or search for particular examples, opinions, or ideas. We can set up a scenario like the highlighter example above, having students working alone, with a partner, and with the whole class, or using different colored flags for different purposes. Remember, we want to teach students to use tools they find appealing and enable them to learn essential skills at the same time.

We can also enrich learning with highlighters, Post-its, and flags by incorporating rubrics to define expectations. By listing categories with varying levels of expectations, rubrics provide specific targets, especially when we include examples. Once students internalize these targets and understand how to seek evidence in a reading, they will be better able to self-assess their progress. Rubric thinking empowers students to know themselves and reduce dependence on feedback from teachers. And, rubrics invite dialogue between teacher and students and thus improve opportunities to learn.

Whenever we take time to teach students how to learn, we smile when we succeed, when we see that they are learning effectively. Sometimes, however, we can feel overwhelmed, thinking we should take on more responsibilities or feel guilty that we have not done enough. Yet, we have to teach our students how to learn: As carpenters need to learn how to use the tools of the trade, so, too, do students. We have the obligation to teach them how to use these tools well.

REFLECTION

Dan Hilliard used to underline in books and write notes in the margins. Recently, however, he decided to use a highlighter and Post-it notes and flags. He particularly likes the flags to indicate key pages. When he realized his students were not using highlighters properly, he decided to create lessons to teach them how to use them well. He also tried out some of his ideas in class about using Post-its and flags. His students seemed to become more curious about what they were reading.

He shared his thinking with Angela, and together they brainstormed other approaches. They also realized that they needed to integrate learning content while introducing these skills. They wanted to be sure students knew what they were learning and why.

POINTS TO PURSUE

☑ Periodically survey your students' knowledge and understandings of how you conduct your classroom, for example, how to prepare for tests, do homework, write papers, discuss, etc. Chances are you will discover misconceptions that you can correct.

☑ Find a one-sheet lesson that appeals to students and use the two-highlighter approach or a variation of your own. Do the exercise several times until students understand how to use the technique well.

☑ Do a similar activity using Post-it notes and flags.

☑ Try homework assignments requiring highlighters, Post-it notes and flags. Assess the homework the following day to reinforce using them well.

☑ Invite students to create a rubric for assessing the use of highlighters, Post-it notes and flags. This is an excellent way to assess their understanding.

☑ Have students create highlighter, Post-it notes, and flags assignments.

☑ Ask colleagues how they use highlighters in their classes. Suggest the ideas from this chapter to those who have not taught the use of highlighters.

CHAPTER 4

Design Invitations

Steve Thomas's students arrive at their classroom door to find all the desks pushed to the side. They hesitate . . .

"Come on in and find a spot on the floor! I've put an intriguing problem on the board for you, one designed to stretch your thinking. I wonder what you will discover! You have the whole period to work on it. You can work alone or with anyone you'd like. You can use any resources in the room or in the library. You can ask me any questions."

Forty minutes later . . .

"For homework, explain to someone at home or in your neighborhood what you did today in class and then come to class tomorrow prepared to write, expressing your thoughts and feelings about what you did—and how you felt about sharing it."

No lecture. No Notes. No roll call.

Steve had wanted to do something like this ever since he saw *Dead Poets Society* over Christmas break. He became fascinated as he watched John Keating (played by Robin Williams) take his students to the trophy room on the first day of school. Steve promised himself he would try something as radical upon returning to school after the New Year.

Steve's yearning to intrigue students to learn illustrates a fundamental responsibility for all of us who teach. As we watch students becoming increasingly uninterested in school, we hear complaints from colleagues. "These kids don't care." "If parents cared, then our students would." "Boys hide inside baggy clothes and girls dress as if they're going to a party." "All they want to do is use their cell phones and iPods." "They never do their homework." We sometimes feel as if we are teaching in a different world, certainly different from the one in which we grew up.

No doubt we are! But, we are still responsible for initiating learning in our classrooms. As much as we might like to disagree, unmotivated students are our responsibility. We cannot give up on any of them until we've done everything possible to intrigue their brains.

Some of them come to us already defeated, having given up hope, believing they are less than smart. We know these kids the moment they walk through the door and watch where they choose to sit. If we give up on them, we put another nail in their coffin, impart another confirmation of their inadequacy, and add another step in their trip towards the street. Rather than appear stupid, they misbehave. We need to begin every beginning—every lesson, every unit, every year—with a commitment to invite students to learn. We not only need to make these invitations intriguing, but also we need to believe in the invitation and its potential. We need, too, to recognize the invitation as our most powerful tool. Threats and coercion have no effect on any student who is convinced that learning in school has no value.

Keating's invitation in *Dead Poets Society* does not focus on learning content (although he employs Robert Herrick's "To the Virgins, to Make Much of Time" as his text) but on the deeper lessons of life he wants his students to pursue in his literature class; he concludes by pointing to old photos of former students and says, "You, too, will soon be pushing up daisies. Carpe Deim, boys. Seize the day!"[18] His students certainly want to return to class the next day, and the next and the next, as Keating's invitation lets them know of his commitment to them and to what they will learn. Steve's invitation, as well, aims to stimulate his students to see the value of open-ended creative problem solving and to trust their own initiative, two of the long-term goals of his teaching.

Teachers love John Keating's foray into the trophy room, but few take time to emulate him. Invitations to learn, after all, take time and require creative juices. Given the pressures to cover material as fast as possible, such invitations cut into teaching time, and losing time creates anxiety. Bariyyah Lawrence told me she stopped teaching fourth grade because she could not get out from under the anxieties she and her students were feeling every day about the MCAS (Massachusetts Comprehensive Assessment System), the state's high stakes test. She feels safer now that she's teaching first grade. So do her children.

Judging from the research and my observations in classrooms, most of us prefer daily routines to assure we can fulfill expectations. At times, we might like to break away, but we hesitate for fear of falling behind or misfiring our creative effort. Yet, some of our colleagues act like John Keating or Steve Thomas every day. Sometimes students arrive in our classrooms buzzing about the crazy thing that just happened in a previous class. We smile, perhaps with a touch of envy, and proceed with our routines. But novelty activates the brain, brain researchers claim. The invigoration of holding hands, for instance, dissipates after a few minutes, just as the scent of perfume quickly recedes. Without novelty in the classroom, we invite boredom. Extending an invitation to learn requires commitment and risk. If we are intrigued but feel resistant, we should engage a colleague to help us design one. Once ready, we should agree to observe each other for support and feedback. If it fails, we will at least have a friend in the house. Our students, as well, might prove supportive if we explain what we attempted and why. They'll probably welcome another try, as novelty is more appealing than routine.

When we make invitations central to our teaching, we begin to see our students as honored guests in our classrooms. Invitations are the most powerful force in teaching. When we use them in our personal lives, we want people to become guests in our homes. When we see our students as guests, we move away from acting as authorities directing from the front of the room. We remember teachers who told us every day where to sit, what to do, when to do it, and how. We complied because this was the way to do school. We now understand that if we continue to espouse learning as compliance, we will fail to teach for such qualities as initiative, responsibility, and creativity—so necessary in our global world.

When we see our students, then, as honored guests (despite their having been assigned to us), we see them as who they are and who they can become. We talk to them as partners in learning rather than act as purveyors of knowledge. We pursue our central question: "What can I do every day to invite children to learn in my classroom?" We see ourselves as hosts serving smorgasbords of ideas, questions, reflections, materials, skills, information, and understandings. We spend our days exchanging rather than telling.

Our decision to extend invitations, however, is the first half of the equation. How students and families respond is the other half. Invitations, like gifts, succeed only when accepted. John Keating's "invitation" worked, as his students accepted his challenge to "seize the day." If our invitations fail, we must persist and feel confident that we can find ones that will work.

Invitational classrooms respect learners with an agreement—an equation—in which teachers engage in a learning exchange with students (and their families). When we decide mainly to talk and deliver, we distort the equation; what students "receive" from us we require them to "give back." They know they must regurgitate what they've "learned" if they are to get an "A," let alone a passing grade.

It's no surprise, then, that students feel increasingly dissatisfied sitting detached in "delivery" classrooms, particularly as they move into middle and high school. Fewer do homework or study for tests. In one school, ninth-grade math teachers told me none of their students would have studied for the mid-term unless the department required a review project. Increasingly, students are not willing to put effort into their work, nor do they care to. As far as most are concerned, school is irrelevant.

When we decide to implement a balanced-equation classroom, we commit not only to bring material to students but also to bring students to the material. We treat content as lumps of clay. We shape opportunities to engage and invite students to re-form it in terms of their understandings. Together we complete the shaping in a deeply creative process. Not only do we develop an understanding of our teaching, but our students also develop their own understandings, which they can take into future learnings. No more constant studying for tests, striving to pass them, and then forgetting everything the next day, as was true for most of us as students.

Creating a classroom culture centered on invitations to learn takes patience, time and persistence. When we apply discipline using consequences rather than punishments, we build trust and confidence by letting students and parents know school will be personal, active, and student-centered, not impersonal, inactive and passive. We become released from the tyranny of teaching-as-talking when we decide to teach by answering the question, "What can I do every day to make learning happen for each and every student in my classroom?" Of course, colleagues might pressure us to abandon such thinking by reminding us, "This is how we do things around here." But once we commit to teaching for learning, we cannot turn back.

We remember our great teachers, because they engaged us. Whatever their teaching styles, we knew we were learning—we felt invited. Even if they lectured, we felt privy to their minds. We learned. Making every moment an invitation to learn opens infinite possibilities. We know we have succeeded when we wake up at the end of class as if in a dream.

"Where did the time go?" we ask. "Where *did* it go?" our students reply.

REFLECTION

Unless we are willing to take responsibility for motivating our students, we may decide not to place much emphasis on intriguing them to learn. We will tend to blame them for being lazy or unwilling learners when, in fact, they may not see the purpose of learning what we want them to. We might be surprised, however, if we raise the ante of expectations by implementing invitations to learn, as Steve Thomas and John Keating demonstrated.

Dan Hilliard's first inclination towards putting his students at the front of his teaching came on the day he sat in Sam's seat in the middle of the room. When he saw *Dead Poets Society*, he vowed someday that he would take such a radical step with his students. But, he wanted to be sure he was not tempted to do it just for show but as integral to what he wanted his students to know, understand, and be able to do.

POINTS TO PURSUE

☑   How important do you think it is to motivate your students? What responsibility do students and parents have for motivation? What is the balance point between the efforts of teachers and students? What can you do to reach this balance point?

☑   Imagine your students as honored guests. What differences would this make? What might you do to let them know? What changes might occur?

☑   Create an invitation to learn for a lesson or unit you have previously taught. Observe any differences you discover.

☑   Ask colleagues what they do to stimulate student interest in learning. Observe them and ask to borrow their ideas, and share yours. Through these exchanges, more students receive the benefits of innovative teaching.

☑   Invite your students to suggest ways to make the classroom more exciting for them. Try their ideas to let them know you listen—and want to learn from them.

☑   Radically rearrange your classroom to surprise students and excite them to learn, as Steve Thomas did in the opening scenario of this chapter. Be sure to have a worthwhile purpose!

CHAPTER 5

Rearrange Rooms

Journal entry:
I step into my first classroom, Room 22, diagonally across from the office. The hanging incandescent-globe lights are off and the room is darkened, as its tan shades are pulled halfway on the tall, multi-paned windows. Desks and chairs are aligned perfectly in rows and columns and face my desk and the blackboard. On my desk sets a new green blotter, a planbook, a class register, a box of Dittos, a box of paperclips, a stapler, two boxes of white chalk, a new eraser and two piles of new textbooks. In the closet behind the desk are sets of older texts, workbooks, miscellaneous texts, and yellow lined-paper full and half-size. The room is clean; these janitors must be good.

I wonder, what will it feel like when my first students walk in next Tuesday? What will it feel like to be at the front of my own room? What will I say? How will students react to this first-year teacher?

That was over forty years ago. Yet, imagine we were Rip Van Winkle and awoke from a one-hundred-year slumber to an unrecognizable world—except for when we stepped into classrooms! The classrooms would have desks in rows and the teacher's desk in front of a whiteboard (which may be still black or green); Venetian blinds perhaps in place of shades on the windows; more than likely, false ceilings with recessed fluorescent lighting; and moveable desks. Rip Van Winkle would immediately know where he was, just as we would immediately recall the regularity of our classrooms. We flash back to the familiar, perhaps remembering where we sat (as I do in Miss Karasack's fourth grade and Miss Mason's sixth). We liked returning to the same seat, our home in the classroom.

We often underestimate the effect of the physical environment on learning. Some of us, such as science teachers with lab stations, have to work within a fixed room design. Most of us, however, have more flexibility than we think, but the traditional nature of "the classroom" has become embedded from years of traditional practice. Perhaps it's time to reconsider how we arrange our learning spaces.

Thus, when we begin from the front of the room on the first day of school, we hardly make a unique impression. And if we are new, we hesitate to be out of step from the norm and not appear as a "real" teacher. So, what can we do to let our students know we do not want to be part of the "the same old, same old?"

If we are stuck with a traditional room arrangement and have to do housekeeping on the first day (pass out forms, registrations, handbooks, schedules, etc.), we can do it in a unique way. We might try to be personable and use a sense of humor, and perhaps, wear a festooned hat or a costume. Or, we might put a query on the board, one to perplex and stimulate their thinking. One of my favorites was giving my eighth graders the "monk on the mountain" problem, which never failed to generate interest, curiosity—and parent involvement as well, a good message in itself. I can't resist including here. (Try to solve it on your own!):

> One morning, exactly at sunrise, a Buddhist monk began to climb a tall mountain. The narrow path, no more than a foot or two wide, spiraled around the mountain to a glittering temple at the summit.
>
> The monk ascended the path at varying rates of speed, stopping many times along the way to rest and to eat the dried fruit he carried. He reached the temple shortly before sunset. After several days of fasting and meditation, he began his journey back along the same path, starting at sunrise and again walking at variable speeds, taking many pauses along the way. His average speed descending was, of course, greater than his average climbing speed.
>
> Prove there is a single spot along the path the monk will occupy on both trips at precisely the same time of day.[19]

If we must use the first day to take care of school business, so be it. Decide, then, to make the next day the tone setter. Be sure students know your intention. As a new teacher, you may not be willing to do what John Keating or Dan Hilliard did, but you should make the experience memorable. One way is to rearrange the desks.

In most schools, classrooms still belong to individual teachers. Unless we share a room, we can choose how to arrange it. We can either use it as we find it, most likely desks in rows and columns, or we can rearrange it. Before we decide, especially for our first impression, we need to be clear in our minds why we are rearranging. If we want students to understand that sitting face-to-face is more important than only facing the backs of the heads of classmates and the teacher (as Dan Hilliard chose), a circular arrangement would make sense. We should prepare a lesson that necessitates this arrangement; otherwise, it might appear gimmicky.

Regardless of what we decide, we need to let go of the traditional classroom mindset. This arrangement has been the staple of classrooms for generations and signifies the teacher as authority, controller, and dispenser. Setting permanent clusters of desks, which are common in elementary schools, also perpetuates the teacher's traditional role. The best alternative is to develop a variety of arrangements to suit the intended learning.

Possible arrangements include facing the front for giving instructions or demonstrations, listening to student presentations, or watching a DVD. But, we do not have to use rows and columns. We can make two or three horseshoe rows to allow for interaction. We also can create clusters of desks for group work, spread them out for quiet study, and push them to the sides to open the middle of the room. In my experience, tables proved more useful than desks, especially trapezoids, which facilitate a wide variety of arrangements. Most of us shy away from rearranging furniture, particularly during class, because we believe it wastes time and creates chaos. So, we make do, leaving the room either as we found it, or keep it arranged the way we've set it.

But again, as in introducing 10-2 Thinking (see Chapter 1), we realize we can take control of our physical space by moving desks. We can take time to teach students to do it effectively and efficiently. The first attempts might well be messy, but rest assured it will work.

Here's a possible scenario:

1. Put a diagram of an alternative arrangement of desks on the board (or on a piece of chart paper, or on an overhead or PowerPoint slide) and ask the students to move their desks into the new arrangement. Time them.

2. After they finish, tell them how long it took. Then ask them to return the desks to the original arrangement, this time without talking.

3. Then, ask them to repeat the new rearrangement without talking. If other classes have done it, you may want to tell them the time to beat. Time them again.

4. Repeat this a few times to reduce the time and the noise to an acceptable level. Again, you may want to say how quickly another group has done it, since students enjoy competition.

5. Whenever you want a different arrangement, you can invoke this procedure more efficiently.

6. Each time you establish a procedure to move desks, it becomes part of your classroom culture. (Putting tennis balls on the feet of desks and chairs reduces noise.)

Moving desks not only facilitates teaching but also sends the message we intend to include students in the ownership of the class. It can also help to alleviate boredom and activate their brains. And, it provides novelty to stimulate thinking. Teaching them how to move the desks helps learning-disabled students, in particular, who need environmental predictability: When they participate in creating the changes, they can understand the "consistencies" of the different arrangements. I know of a teacher who has several different seating charts on her wall; she simply points to the one she wants her children to use, and they quickly rearrange the room.

Some teachers may hesitate to use this practice, afraid that students will not work well in groups or will waste time unless they are facing us. Yet, those students who have difficulty in groups may well be the same ones who feign paying attention when sitting and "listening." As in introducing any procedure, however, we need to believe in it and then teach it until it is learned. If our intention is to involve students in what they do during class, we can be confident in our approach. And, when they are not in rows, how delightful for them to be able to look at each other instead of the backs of heads!

Recently, I came across an account of a school in Minnesota that experimented with stand-up desks in some upper grade classrooms. Based on stand-up workstations in adult workplaces, students can either stand or sit on barstool-height chairs.[20] I imagined how helpful such an approach would have been for me, given how antsy I was in school—and how many of my middle-school students would have enjoyed it. Whenever I offered students options to work away from their desks, many took advantage—sometimes working on the floor—and were usually productive.

Another option few teachers have chosen to create an engaging learning environment is to forsake desks entirely. Instead, they create a non-traditional classroom using chairs, couches, desks, tables, plants, photos, artwork, and low tables. Upon entering, students almost forget they are in school. These rooms can feel structured yet relaxed, open and focused, certainly alive and comfortable. The message asserts that all are welcome—each person including the teacher has a personal space. By not "being school," it eliminates the habitual expectations of the traditional classroom. How refreshing, instead, to feel invited into conversation, dialogue, and originality—and with high standards.

When we choose to teach from the middle of the room, we stand at the front when we need to. We ask the whole class to pay attention only when necessary. We rearrange spaces to facilitate learning. We integrate the physicality of the room to match the flexibility we expect of our students and ourselves. We invoke a fundamental principle of teaching to facilitate learning in spaces designed to promote our intentions.

REFLECTION

On the day Dan Hilliard sat in Sam's seat, he had his first inkling of what it means to teach from the middle of the room. He sensed the potential of students' learning among themselves—an extension of a process he had been developing from the front of the room. The next day he returned to his traditional position at the front but was determined to continue to experiment.

A week later, he decided to try shifting desks partway through the period. He began the lesson showing a DVD clip that he stopped periodically to generate interest and discussion. Once done, he put a diagram on the board to share how he wanted the desks rearranged. He knew it would be somewhat confusing, but the process went fairly well. He thanked his students and said that tomorrow they would become more efficient at moving desks. For the rest of the lesson, he presented a problem for each group to solve based on the DVD.

Taking the first step opens possibilities. The next steps develop from responses to the first. Teaching and learning may never be the same.

POINTS TO PURSUE

☑ If you intend to make your first day unique, seek the advice of others who do the same. Search Google for ideas.

☑ As a precursor to moving desks during a class period, reset them in different ways on different days for a week or two. (Be sure to inform inclusion students who might react anxiously to the changes.) Then, shifting during class may not seem as disruptive. Or, take a risk—put an alternative scheme on the board or on chart paper for the arrangement of desks in your room, and try the procedures outlined in this chapter.

☑ Be clear about why you need to rearrange the room whenever you decide. Don't be intimidated by students' resistance, as they are as accustomed to desks in rows and columns as you are. Sometimes, our "best" students resist the most.

☑ Pay attention to how rearrangements affect student learning—teachable moments perhaps?

☑ If other teachers have arranged desks differently or rearrange them during class, observe and ask them about how and why they implemented this.

CHAPTER 6

Make Meaning

"Here's an index card for each of you. On one side please write down three new ideas you learned from our discussion today. On the other, please write a question you think we should pursue to better understand what we are learning.

"You do not need to put your name on the card. I will use these to assess what we accomplished and where we might take our work from here."

When we shift from talking *at* students to talking *with* them, we see them learning *in the classroom*. We pay attention to what works and what does not—and we keep an open mind. We listen more. We see them engaged and retaining more of what we teach, so we seek other strategies. We investigate the Internet and educational publications. We rearrange the room as needed. We ask colleagues for their ideas and practices. Teachers at my workshops are frequently surprised by how much they learn from fellow participants.

We can begin by envisioning teaching as giving piano lessons. We need to see ourselves as the piano teacher who invites her students to play alongside her, giving feedback, and sending them home with new skills to practice. If she simply demonstrated how the keys moved, identified the notes she played, pointed to the score, and so on, her students would leave without any techniques and skills to try on their own.

Engaging students in activities with purpose is essential. Not to do so leads to doing activities for their own sake. As interesting and fun as they may be, when activities fail to connect to a larger purpose, we waste valuable time. When we implement the four strategies outlined in this chapter, we find ourselves teaching from the middle of the room, literally and metaphorically. *Exit Cards, Recap Cards,* and *Give One/Get One* are interactive and instructional. The fourth strategy, the *TAPS Template for Teacher Planning,* assures that our lessons and units lead to coherent and sensible learning.

Exit Cards

Every day, we face students in our classrooms. How often do we ask them how well we (or they) are doing? Why do some of us wait until the end of the year to ask for evaluations from our students about our teaching? Why are we chained to the oft-dreaded feedback from a supervisor's formal evaluation (often a dog-and-pony show that has little to do with what we do everyday)? Why are we hesitant to invite colleagues to observe and critique our teaching?

Exit Cards can help us break through this lack of effective feedback and help us improve our teaching. They are quick to use. We simply pass out index cards, ask for questions or comments, and collect them. I first learned about Exit Cards from Grant Wiggins when he shared a story about a teacher who used them every Friday. We can use them after a lesson, a unit of study, in the middle of a block period—any time we want.

When using Exit Cards in my workshops with teachers, I usually ask two questions, one for each side of the card, such as:

"What worked for you today?" and "What question do you need an answer to?"
"I like . . ." and "I wish . . ."
"What do you think was the big idea of today's lesson?" and "What question do you have?"
Or, simply, "Anything I need to know to teach better or help you learn?"

It is better not to ask negative questions, such as, "What didn't you like?" or "What did not work?" I have found they encourage venting rather than provide constructive comments.

Exit Cards work because they're immediate and anonymous. Certainly, we might receive anomalies, as I did from a disgruntled participant who did not want to attend my professional development workshop in the first place: "*I like* that this workshop is over," he wrote. "*I wish* that we did not have any more." Interestingly enough, when I shared this comment, people immediately recognized who wrote it; eventually, I was able to befriend this person and hopefully was able bring him into the mix of the conversation.

Exit Cards allow us to ascertain patterns as to what's working (we can do more of the same); what's troublesome (we can respond and change); and to gain insights (we discover new ideas). I usually share what I learned from the Exit Cards at the next session to demonstrate their value (indicating how I may have changed my plans) and to encourage thoughtful feedback.

I wish I had used them with my students. Had I done so, I would have assigned a specific color to each class, or to each subject area in a self-contained classroom; the different colors would have made it easier to focus on each class or subject. While some students would surely have dismissed them, I imagine most comments would have yielded valuable insights. Overall, they would have provided me with consistent feedback.

Most often, I imagine using them anonymously, but it might be useful to have students sign their names, for example, to know their interest in particular topics, or to assign them to interest groups the next day. Given that it takes about two minutes to fill them out and not much longer to read, Exit Cards are a wise investment.

Recap Cards

As Exit Cards provide instant feedback about our teaching, students also should have immediate feedback about to their learning before they leave class. Recap Cards give them opportunities to test their knowledge, skills, and understandings during the last ten minutes of class.[21] Instead of relying on "Thumbs up; thumbs down," or asking, "How many of you think you know . . . ?" or calling on a few students to get a quick reading, Recap Cards make *every* student process the day's lesson—and receive immediate feedback.

This is the procedure for using Recap Cards:[22]

1. With about ten minutes of class time remaining, give each student a standard-lined index card (3 x 5 or 4 x 6).
2. Have students write a recap of the most important points in the lesson or solve the assessment problem of the day. Make sure they put their name on the card.
3. Instruct students to pass the cards to peers in their cooperative

learning group. Be sure to change the groupings bi-weekly to ensure that each student will receive a wide range of opinions.

4. Have peers rate the recap according to a predetermined rubric (see below) for good communication. Have the reviewers place their initials against the rating. Record the peer evaluation values.

5. Return the reviewed index recaps to the authors. Have a student or two who score three stars from their peers share their responses. If time permits, discuss the ratings and how the recaps can be made stronger. Periodically post examples of excellent recaps or place them on an overhead next to the rubric.

This is a rubric that was used in math classes:[23]

- Three Stars is given to a recap that is clear, accurate, grasps the main ideas of the lesson, and shows how the problem was solved.

- Two stars indicate a satisfactory job of getting the main idea, but the response was either unclear to the reader or had several errors. The response showed only a basic understanding of the ideas involved.

- One star shows an attempt at the problem, but it is hard to read, not very clear, or had several errors. The response shows only a basic understanding of the ideas involved.

- Zero stars reflects major errors in understanding the ideas.

What a gift to students to see what they've learned at a lesson. What a gift to the teacher to know how well each student learned.[24]

Gathering data from Exit Cards proves invaluable in our efforts to engage and make connections as we move away from the front of the room. Recap Cards help students (and us) assess both what we teach and what they learn. These two are only samples of summarizers that can provide valuable formative feedback. Among the most useful are:

- *Envelope Please and Crumple and Toss*: similar to Exit Cards but with a twist. Ask students the same types of questions and either put the cards into an envelope or toss them into a basket. Using the envelope allows students to write questions about the lesson. After checking them over, teachers can pass the questions back randomly the next day for peers to answer.

- *3-2-1*: for example, 3 big ideas about . . . , 2 problems you see, and 1 question you want answered.[25]

- *The Important Thing*: create a brochure applying evidence about a lesson, based on Margaret Wise Brown's *Important Book* (Harper and Row, 1949).[26]

- *The One-Minute Paper*: a popular higher-education tool used at the end of lectures, in which students answer, "What is the big point you learned in class today?" and "What is the main unanswered question for you from today's class?"[27]

- *Ticket to Leave*: another term for Exit Card. I have used the term Ticket to Leave when asking teachers to declare their particular interest in a future topic that we'll investigate. In planning a jigsaw on brain research, for example, my colleague, Pam Penna, invites participants to rank order the five topics they'll consider and place them accordingly into groups.

Give One/Get One

Give One/Get One (or as some middle school colleagues prefer: Seek One/Share One), offers an invaluable way to activate students to learn from one another. Using the Give One/Get One form, I ask teachers in my workshops first to write approaches that they use to reach challenging students in the top three boxes; then, they move around the room to share their approaches and gather ideas from colleagues, then put ideas in the bottom six boxes. (See a Sample Use of Give One/Get One in Figure 6.1.) Invariably, teachers pick up new ideas from one another, have an opportunity to share their thinking—and they also enjoy the process.

Give One/Get One What can you do to help all students be successful in your classroom— especially the most difficult and challenging students?		
I contact parents early in the year to tell them something good about their child.	I place students near where I can see them.	I set up a private signal to let John know when I can see that he is about to cause trouble for himself.
Set up a parent conference and include a guidance counselor.	Create exciting material that appeals to the most resistant learner.	Provide physical space and room to move for Bill to help him focus. It usually works.
See Ross Greene's "Three Baskets" from his book The Explosive Child: sort out handling meltdowns; high priority behaviors we work out, and low priority ones we can remove from our radar screen.	Take time to discuss patterns of class behavior to teach and reinforce a respectful classroom; be willing to take time to do this, or nothing will be learned.	Assume that the student does not know how to do something rather than that he does not want to do it.

Figure 6.1.
Sample Use of Give One/Get One.[28]

Give One/Get One encourages community building, as it opens people to learn from one another. It also builds confidence, as they see others writing down their ideas. And, it builds collective responsibility for learning the material in question. Like all new procedures, we should take time to teach our students how to interact using Give One/Get One.

Another Give One/Get One approach helps students review and prepare for a test (Figure 6.2). Instead of reviewing material *for* students, we can set up "Give One/Get One as Review" to invite them to review independently, with each other, and then as a class. The opportunity to interact lets them, and us, know what they think they need to learn. They do the work of the review, and better still, we do not have to "go over" what will be on the test.

We can use Give One/Get One at any time during a lesson. Some teachers use it to pre-assess students' knowledge, understandings, and skills. Others have used it in the middle of a lesson to stimulate sharing of ideas or to answer questions. And some use it at the end as a summarizer. As with other interactive strategies, we need to use it in context of what we want students to know, understand, and be able to do. Otherwise it becomes another gimmick. The TAPS Template that follows assures that we teach meaningfully.

TAPS Template for Teacher Planning

This last strategy demonstrates the importance of integrating interactive methods, such as those in this chapter, within a clear, well-defined context. The TAPS Template for Teacher Planning builds on Grant Wiggins and Jay McTighe's Backwards Design structure (with some input from Chip and Dan Heath), and Carol Ann Tomlinson's Differentiated Instruction methods (Figure 6.3). When using this template for planning, we commit to the fundamental elements of successful instruction, and at the same time, avoid teaching a series of disconnected lessons as happens, for example, when we rely on textbook chapters for our curriculum.

Unlike the strategies discussed thus far, the TAPS Template for Teacher Planning requires careful attention to every part of a lesson, unit, and course of study. For example, we need to develop effective

✔ Pass out a Give One/Get One sheet (designed in any way you'd like).

✔ Begin by asking students to fill in three blanks with what they think will be important to learn for the upcoming test.

✔ Have them leave their desks to gather ideas from their classmates.

✔ Whenever they find that others have the same idea(s), they should put that person's initials on their sheet in the corresponding box; the others should do the same on their sheets.

✔ When they find a new idea, they put it in a blank box. Once they have all boxes filled in, they return to their seats.

✔ Ask the class to share first those items that have the most number of initials on their Give One/Get One sheets. This way, the most common ideas will be collected first. Record these on the board.

✔ Then ask students to share ideas that they feel are important, even though no one else listed the same idea. Put these on the board, unless it is obvious they should not be added.

✔ Add a couple of essentials of your own if they do not come from students.

✔ Make up (or modify) the test based on what's on the board! Why?

- Students are empowered because they have a say in what needs to be learned.

- Teachers discover what students have learned, which may or may not be what the teachers had intended.

✔ Ultimately, as a teacher, you are acting like a coach; that is, you are using the material that will be used in the "game" (test). No more guessing games! Students study what they need to study.

Figure 6.2.
Give One/Get One as Review.

How does this lesson connect to the core idea of this unit? What will students know, understand, or be able to do as a result of this lesson? How does it connect to the previous and the next lessons?

What essential questions might you ask to drive the thinking? For example, "What do you notice?" and "What do you wonder?"

How will you activate the lesson, intrigue students to want to learn it? What mystery could you create? What surprise might you use? Is there a story you could relate?

Format	Used for
Total Class	• Directions • 10-2 Thinking • Video viewing • Give One/Get One . . .
Alone	• Journal writing • Quizzes • Reflections . . .
Pairs*	• Peer review • Think-pair-share • Clock partners . . .
Small Groups	• Tiered instruction • Interest groups • Give One/Get One • Anchoring activities . . .

How will you and your students know what they are learning?

How will students summarize the learning (for example, using Exit and Recap Cards)?

What homework (home-practice) will you give to connect and intrigue students?

*You can put students into groups of three if you prefer. Trios work as well as pairs in pair-designed exercises.

Figure 6.3.
TAPS Template for Teacher Planning.

essential questions, such as these from the Math Forum at Drexel University: "What do you notice?" "What do you wonder?"[29] Such questions must be developed with a thorough understanding of the intended lesson or unit. As with all good teaching, we can change some practices more easily than others. The TAPS Template for Teacher Planning includes elements of teaching we may already do well, but applying all of them into a coherent structure demands time, patience, collaboration, and hard work.

When we plan with all of the *T*, *A*, *P*, and *S* elements of the template, we diversify our teaching to meet the flexible needs of students and avoid relying on only one-size-fits-all, whole-class lessons. As we apply the template in designing lessons, we need to keep two questions in mind about our students:

Who's not going to get it?
Who will get it quickly or already know it?

Once these questions become embedded in our minds, we can never again assume all students will learn in the same way at the same pace. As we plan, we will think about how each individual learns.

Implementing the TAPS Template for Teacher Planning assures us that we will teach coherent, aligned, and relevant material. It assures, as well, when we use pedagogies such as Exit Cards, Recap Cards, and Give One/Get One, they will serve purposeful learning. We always improve our chances to make learning possible whenever we place the context of a lesson within the scheme of our intentions—and when we diversify how we present the learning. Committing to the TAPS Template for Teacher Planning gives us the rich opportunity to teach from the middle of the room while making coherent, aligned learning happen in our classrooms every day.

REFLECTION

Those of us who have been teaching for a while may never have heard about the ideas described in this chapter. It takes about thirty years for good ideas to become common practice in the classroom, as it took thirty years after the Wright Brothers developed flight to implement commercial flying.

Ever since Dan Hilliard heard the metaphor linking the piano teacher to the classroom teacher, he has committed to concentrate on student learning in every lesson. Techniques, such as Exit Cards, Recap Cards, and Give One/Get One, have improved his ability to assess and to redesign his teaching to meet his students' needs. Dan decided to hold a best-practices conversation with colleagues every on the third Thursday of the month. So far, five of his colleagues have joined and others have expressed interest, as well.

It behooves us to become alert to new and better ways to teach and learn. By implementing the ideas in this chapter, we will improve our repertoire, and more importantly, begin to nurture our commitment to let go of traditional practices that no longer work. We develop new habits of teaching.

POINTS TO PURSUE

☑ Begin making it a practice to use Exit Cards and Recap Cards. Don't worry if students do not take them seriously at first. If you persist, they will.

☑ Design a Give One/Get One exercise to activate your students learning either before, during, or at the end of a unit. Take your time to integrate this process.

☑ Explore the TAPS Template for Teacher Planning to see how it relates to how you plan. Be patient as you attend to each part and recognize it will take time to internalize its structure. Try its framework (begin focusing on a particular part if you prefer) to see how it helps you connect the various elements of your teaching. Ask colleagues if they know how to use the elements of the TAPS Template. Search Google as well. See if using the TAPS Template improves student learning. Pay attention to student responses as you implement it.

☑ Begin a conversation around implementing the strategies in this chapter, particularly the TAPS Template for Teacher Planning.

☑ Develop a seminar for you and your colleagues to discuss and implement the ideas in this chapter—and the ideas and practices in all of Part I.

PART II

How Can We Develop Our Teaching Practice?

Once we begin to shift our practices towards the middle of the room, we begin to think differently about our roles. We feel differently as well. Seeing students respond as we listen and teach encourages us to try more new ideas and approaches. If we intend to grow and expand, we need to reflect and consider broader perspectives on teaching and learning. We must also look within and beyond if we are to discover and nurture our practice.

The ideas in Part II invite us first to step back and assess the big picture. Despite the isolated nature of the classroom, we cannot ignore the larger factors governing our world and causing rapid change. Nor can we ignore our own thought processes as we mature in our teaching. We need to find ways to stay abreast of current innovative thinking in our field.

Ultimately, we need to examine the full range of our practices by asking hard questions to determine what we need to change to meet the needs and demands of our students, their families, and the global world in which we live. We, then, need to commit to making these changes happen.

CHAPTER 7

See the Big Picture

We learn to teach by osmosis. From our earliest days in school, we absorb the habits and practices of our teachers who, in turn, learned to teach from their teachers standing at the front of the class, delivering one-size-fits-all whole-class lessons, using textbooks, taking attendance, filling out plan books, averaging grades, assigning homework, and keeping kids after school—and doing it alone.

In the process we internalize notions about good teaching without much scrutiny. For instance, a history teacher develops the notion that he needs to be able to answer any student question, when in fact he might better stimulate thinking by conjuring "unanswerable" questions. Or more likely, he believes his students must take notes every day to learn what he knows, rather than seek answers to authentic, worthwhile questions from widely available resources, thus inviting thinking into the classroom.

Or, a math teacher who internalized one way of learning math as a pupil now repeats the same pattern with her students. She begins each class by having students put homework on the board, corrects the examples, and collects the homework. She teaches a new concept, and then allows time to start the homework assignment before the bell rings. Had her math teachers allowed time in class for her and her peers to invent solutions to problems and present them to the class for scrutiny, for example, she might have become a different—and better—math teacher.

Habitual practices can constrict us from seeing other possibilities. Many of us internalize the weekly approach to lesson planning as the proper way to prepare. Friday is test day, we deliver material Monday through Wednesday, and use Thursday for review. We've sat through countless such classes, so it's no wonder many of us replicate this practice. This routine, which appears sensible on the surface, fragments thinking and learning, because it does not allow for flexibility and in-depth exploration. It is, however, the perfect coverage methodology. And, we can say we've done our job.

As we pay attention to our established practices, we begin to see the effects of what we do. For example, we might recognize our part in the failure of students to do homework rather than simply blaming them. We could, then, redefine homework as home-practice and offer options, such as allowing students to pick six of ten questions they believe will help them learn best or to create their own questions and answers. We might invite them to answer selected questions or create a graphic organizer to illustrate their understandings. Or, we might ask them to decide what they plan to do for homework.

We need to reexamine our habitual practices, because unlike generations of teachers before us, we teach into an unknown cultural future. Given the quickening pace of the doubling of knowledge, the plethora of new technologies, and the ubiquitous access to the Internet, we cannot act as if the world will be as it was when we were in school. We need to awaken and respond to our media-driven culture and plunge into its mix keeping our minds and hearts open. If we cling to unconscious teaching habits, we will soon face obsolescence, as students will surely look for learning elsewhere. Becoming bored with us, they will further immerse themselves into technology's instant capacity to connect them with whatever they see. We will be shut out.

Given present uncertainties, we should drive our teaching towards discovering new possibilities. We will better serve our students by steering them towards tasks with which they will have to struggle to learn and complete (a concept unknown to many of them!), and by teaching them to live with the questions rather than jump to quick answers. We cannot do this unless we are willing to let go of our teaching comforts and routines and become willing to struggle ourselves.

How will we change? We can begin by taking time to reexamine the contexts in which we teach and determine how we can begin to collaborate effectively. As we accept the changing world, we discover new perspectives that open us to rethink what we do and need to do. The three ideas in this chapter offer you ways to consider the implications of the world we are growing into.

The Big Shift

Whenever I conduct workshops, I provide at least one opportunity to consider the wider perspective of our work. One of my favorites I have entitled *The Big Shift* (Figure 7.1). I invite someone to read it aloud. I then ask people to pair up with someone with whom they do not work or do not know and discuss these three questions:

1. What do you notice to be different about today's students?
2. How have you changed your teaching in response (if you have)?
3. As a result of discussing The Big Shift, what might you do differently?

Sometimes, I ask each pair to join another pair and decide on one big idea to bring back to their table groups. Each table then decides on what they believe is important to share with the workshop. I observe and listen to intense exchanges and arguments about to the truths of The Big Shift. Everyone recognizes that we teach in a different culture today, and will need to find ways to respond effectively. What we decide to do, however, depends on us.

I sometimes bring up Richard Lavoie's three words defining the way we now live: "Unlearn, Learn, Relearn." Citing the example of the telephone, Lavoie traces our relationship from the rotary phone to the iPhone.[30] In nearly all aspects of our culture, we need to unlearn what we learned in order to learn anew just to keep up (for example, cooking, cell phones, computers, GPS, TiVo/DVR, Amazon's Kindle, iPad) and once we've finally learned, a new "model" appears, and unless we decide to update, our "old model" soon becomes obsolete. This way of living is natural for the young, but a struggle for most of us.

How People Learn

Another handout I frequently use invites participants to examine their teaching practices in light of a summary, *How People Learn*, which replicates a well-known pyramid describing retention levels when

Whether we want to admit it or not, we are in the midst of a huge cultural shift in our society. Some have called these times of change as significant as the Renaissance—and others say more so!

This shift is evident in the exponential expansion of the media both in content and technologies. These effects are most obvious in the children we are now being asked to teach.

We are at the vortex of this radical shift in our culture. Unless we respond with intelligence, creativity and commitment, our students will zoom past us ignoring our outmoded methods and approaches. They will find ways to educate themselves, as have all pioneers who invent solutions to newfound problems.

"Our students have changed radically," says Marc Prensky. "Today's students are no longer the people our educational system was designed to teach."*

We need to examine our current purposes and practices in light of the information-age culture. We cannot remain in isolated classrooms. Students cannot be expected to work in isolation either. Instead, as we move toward collaboration and cooperation, our students will need to be encouraged and supported in working together to learn. Already, they are instant messaging homework—and some with their teachers! Individual accountability will remain, yes, but it will come to mean something different. What, we are not sure.

We will need to collaborate and to create ways for meeting today's students where they are and nurture them to become good students, good citizens, and good people. This is not about indulging them. We have much to offer—and we need to decide just what that is.

*Quote from: Marc Prensky, "Digital Natives, Digital Immigrants."

Figure 7.1.
The Big Shift.

learning (Figure 7.2). Most teachers have seen this information in one form or another and usually nod their heads in quick agreement and want to move on.

When I first used a similar chart, I indicated that students learn better when actively engaged and left it at that. Later, I decided to add the bold line between "See and Hear" and "Say" to have teachers consider its implications more closely. By asking them to pair up and sometimes regroup into fours (as we did with The Big Shift), I set in motion similar rigorous conversations around the essential elements of effective teaching.

I provide questions to consider about How People Learn, such as:

What does this chart indicate as to how you distribute your instruction practice both above and below the line?

Is below-the-line teaching "better" than above-the-line teaching?

Can we teach only from either above the line or below the line?

How accurate do you think the percents are as stated in the chart? Are they accurate for you?

What other questions does the chart raise?

I stress the huge implications when we pay attention to the structure of the chart: By assessing How People Learn, we are compelled to focus on learning. We realize that we cannot stay in the delivery mode. We quickly understand that staying above the line means primarily to teach from the front of the room, whereas distributing teaching above and below the line enables us to move into the middle. We also discuss that the averages cited do not apply to all people.

For most of us, however, the idea of "spending time below the line" presents two challenges. First, students might teach each other "wrong" information, and second, it takes more time. When we stay above the line, in contrast, we can be sure students are hearing "correct" information, and it allows us to cover the ever-enlarging amount of material required. This thinking assumes that students learn as we explain. Furthermore, it means we cannot monitor what students will teach one another, when in fact we should be involved closely in that process. For instance, before students teach, we can ask them to write what they intend to share. Not only can we assess their thinking, but

People learn . . .

- 10% of what they READ

- 20% of what they HEAR

- 30% of what they SEE

- 50% of what they both SEE and HEAR

- 70% of what they SAY

- 80% of what they EXPERIENCE

- 90% of what they SAY and DO

- 95% of what they TEACH

Figure 7.2.

How People Learn.

A common chart or pyramid that teachers learn about in education courses looks something like this one.

(This particular chart has been adapted from charts by Edgar Dale, Eldon Ekwall and James L. Shanker, William Glasser, and David Sousa. While the original source of the research is unclear, it provides for stimulating conversation about how people learn, particularly when I add the bold line.)

we also provide time to develop their writing skills. It may be more time consuming than delivering, but it is more effective, more enduring—and more responsible.

Entity Theory versus Incremental Theory of Learning

A third big idea that forces us to rethink how we perceive student learning potential derives from the work of Jeff Howard, which I first learned about from John Saphier. Saphier's chart emphasizes Howard's understanding of the distinction between fixed and fluid intelligence. It articulates *Entity Theory*, the bell curve based on IQ that determines fixed intelligence levels of students, versus *Incremental Theory*, which is based on Howard's fluid concept of Effective Effort to enable students to "get smarter" (Figure 7.3).

The concept of fixed intelligence based on the bell curve formed the basis for the factory-model schools of the past century. Young children were sorted out by IQ and put in leveled classes throughout their school years. We now know, however, that natural intelligence indicates a small fraction of future success. Daniel H. Pink concludes that IQ counts for the entry point into fields of study but has a four to ten percent effect on success.[31] Jonah Lehrer makes a compelling argument that self-control has a greater effect on academic success than IQ.[32] "Smart is not something you are. Smart is something you get," the mantra of Jeff Howard's Efficacy Institute, is a prime example of the incremental theory in practice.[33] As teachers, we would be wise not to assume the entity level of anyone's intelligence but teach keeping in mind Incremental Theory. Nothing less is acceptable.

We can build confidence in students by using errors as feedback rather than as indicators of low intelligence. Using this frame of mind, we can suspend prejudgments about students based on grouping or tracking and instead concentrate on their potential and provide multiple pathways for getting smarter.[34] We can, in Saphier and Gower's words, help students "exceed expectations"[35] by invoking Saphier's dictum:

"This is important."

"You can do it."

"I will not give up on you."[36]

Belief #1. The Entity Theory

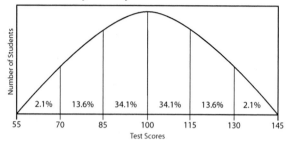

Characterized by such assumptions as

- Intelligence determines learning and achievement.
- Intelligence is: one essence; fixed (can't get smarter); innate (inherited); measurable.
- Failure to achieve is explained largely by lack of intelligence.

Belief #2. The Incremental Theory

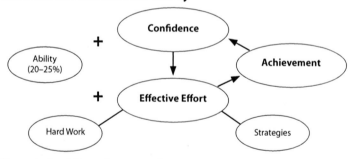

Characterized by such assumptions as

- Intelligence is not fixed; it is possible to "get smarter."
- Innate ability explains only a part of learning and achievement.
- Intelligent behavior such as the use of strategies or self-monitoring and correction can be taught and practiced.
- Failure to achieve is an opportunity to adjust and try again.

Figure 7.3.
Two Beliefs about Intelligence and Achievement.

(Adapted from the work of Jeff Howard, Founder and President of the Efficacy Institute, and John Saphier, President of Research for Better Teaching.)

Without a doubt, invoking the Incremental Theory has profound implications to our teaching in every lesson, every day. When we apply the Entity-Theory, we deprive students of realizing their potential, no matter how we rationalize. When we think we know a student's limitations, we send a message he is less than he might be. When we organize our schools around "ability levels," we invite either false assumptions about "high-level" students' "brightness," or, perhaps the more insidious, "low-level" students' inferiorities.[37]

When we keep in mind The Big-Shift perspective, understand How People Learn, and adopt the Incremental Theory mindset, we become open to see that *every* student is capable of reaching the stars, rather than a select few.

REFLECTION

Taking the longer view and exploring the big picture requires time. Unless we are willing to take this step, we may find ourselves becoming obsolete inside a rapidly changing culture. Students wired for digital thinking will reject our efforts to dispense knowledge and skills in the old ways. We need to find our bearings in this new world and bring our intelligence, skills, and wisdom into the classroom.

Dan Hilliard has the insatiable curiosity of Rudyard Kipling's "elephant's child." He asked more questions than anyone in his family. Sometimes, he would ask a second question without waiting to hear the answer to the first. As a teacher, he discovered that this curiosity led him to try new ideas and take risks. Sometimes, he got into trouble. Early in his career he decided to give all students in his "top" section an "A" for the year on the first day of school. He stuck to his commitment despite the chagrin of the guidance counselor.

He has become fascinated by today's fast-changing culture, particularly as it affects his students. He tries to imagine how he would have grown up in their world.

POINTS TO PURSUE

☑ How can we celebrate the lifestyles of the young? How can we see ourselves growing up inside their world? How can we help them become thoughtful, creative, and civil citizens amidst media pressures to emulate celebrities, watch frivolous television, and listen to misogynous popular music, among other incongruous phenomena?

☑ How can we invoke How People Learn to help us move away from delivery? How can we support students to teach each other well if we feel pressured to cover as much as we can? How do we free ourselves from the hamster-wheel of teaching enough to let our students into the process of creating the equation of learning?

☑ How does the Entity Theory/Incremental Theory continuum affect how you think of students? Do some seem "naturally bright," because of their demeanor? Do others appear "slow" when it may be far from the truth?

☑ If we work in a school that schedules students based on levels (more than likely) how can we overcome its impact on student self-perceptions? How might we begin the process of convincing the school to consider the values of heterogeneous grouping? At least, acknowledging the obvious differences among students, how can we find ways to finally drop such terms as "slow groups," and "low-level learners"?

CHAPTER 8

Search for Wisdom

I shall be telling this with a sigh
Somewhere ages and ages hence:
Two roads diverged in a wood, and I—
I took the one less traveled by,
And that has made all the difference.

(From Robert Frost, "The Road Not Taken")[38]

The mystics see from universal space. The Vedas speak of looking from behind the eyes. The Taoists say the Tao is unnamed, the source from which all emanates. Rumi invites us to "Sell our cleverness and purchase bewilderment." Eckhart Tolle speaks of the Now as the only reality. And, Robert Frost in "The Road Not Taken" voices the teacher-mystic in all of us. Oh, how we choose knowing we might have chosen differently! How we promise ourselves to return but keep on! And, how we look back and see our path as ". . . the one less traveled by/And that has made all the difference."

This poem lives within me. When I first read it, I interpreted Frost as having taken life's less-traveled road. I imagined me, too, on a less traveled road, uncommon to my colleagues—and most pleased with myself! But, later I discovered his real message comes from looking back—"I shall be telling this with a sigh/Somewhere ages and ages hence." We rationalize our having taken a unique path when we had hardly any sense of it beforehand. Frost invites us instead to see our path—our teaching—for what it is rather than for what we think it has been.

We need to recognize and accept the realities of our teaching. While we may or may not take a less traveled road, we become wiser when we take time to reflect on the meaning of the one we chose. Unless we do, we will be denying ourselves access to the deeper meaning of our work. Knowing ourselves, knowing our preferences, after all, informs us of our adventure, one of our own making—and that makes all the difference.

This chapter is personal: I have chosen to reflect on my own experience in hopes that readers will recognize the importance of theirs and choose also to reflect. Although my examples are unique—as anyone's would be—I imagine we all share similar patterns and sources.

When I began teaching, I immersed myself in the myriad, overwhelming tasks of keeping up with the expected and unexpected. I applied my own sense of teaching and experimented with new ideas, particularly from co-teaching with my department head. But, it was not until years later that I allowed larger perspectives into my life and teaching. I discovered not only the joy of learning the wisdom of the "greats" but also the gifts they brought. I explored texts from the *Tao Te Ching*, Confucius, the Buddha, Jesus and writings by Thich Nhat Hanh, Dalai Lama, Jon Kabat-Zinn, Wendell Berry, Rumi, and Hafiz, among many others. Some have become seminal influences and forever changed my practice.

I cannot count the times these teachings energized my classroom and enriched my teaching. Despite pressures from an expanding media-centered culture, encroaching state and school authorities, and unrealistic expectations of parents, I came to understand (before I think I recognized it) that my primary responsibility was to teach to the interior landscape of each and every child, to meet their human longing to understand themselves and their place in the universe—the place where the ancient sages dwelled.

I discovered the depth of this truth when teaching Ancient History later in my career. The school required that I use a textbook to provide the basics to prepare daily lessons, give quizzes and tests, assign papers and homework, and determine grades. The students, then, would have "covered" Ancient History and been "prepared" for the next year. No one would have argued had I done just that. Students would not have complained either, other than the usual gripes of eighth-graders. After all, they were used to the culture of the textbook, since this was how they had been trained. This is a pattern teachers know and use well— or not, depending upon one's point of view.

Such limited teaching, however, does not satisfy. We yearn for meaningful classrooms in which learning happens by invitation within the context of rich and worthwhile material. Sometimes we succeed, other times we come up short. Often, we hesitate for fear that we'll fall behind in what we think we need to cover. But, when we are willing to take the risk, we can achieve the unexpected.

Rather than relying on the textbook's narrative on ancient China, I collected primary sources on the analects of Confucius, chapters of the *Tao Te Ching*, and sutras of the Buddha. In addition, we read Benjamin Hoff's *The Tao of Pooh* and readings from the Dalai Lama. After thoughtful conversations over several weeks, I asked my students to make an imaginary journey to China to seek the wisdom of the ancients, then write an essay reflecting their thoughts on one of the following questions of their choice:

How am I to understand and better myself?
How am I to live within my family so peace and harmony prevail?
How am I to relate to others so goodness prevails?
How am I to live well within nature and the environment?

I wanted my students to discover their own understandings and to apply the wisdom of the ancients to support their conclusions. I asked them to dwell within their interior landscape and discover their own truths. I also asked them not to seek out other sources, but to reexamine and explore those we had explored and discussed.

By the time students completed their journey and reported their findings, many realized that they had seen themselves in a new light, often with astonishment. They sensed the generosity of the assignment. "I thought I knew myself before writing this paper," Dorsey wrote, "but now I understand myself differently and more clearly. Thank you, Mr. Thoms."

This assignment, developed over several years, succeeded because:

- It tapped into core human concerns.

- It evoked a passion for seeking wisdom and relating it to students' lives.

- It put fundamental human qualities at the forefront including civility, kindness, generosity, thankfulness, helpfulness, self-awareness, competence, hope, truth, wisdom, engagement, respect, responsibility, care, compassion, communication, and empathy.

• It demanded probing discussions, rigorous reading and rereading, writing and rewriting. I assessed students' drafts on my computer each night and returned them to their files on the school's network, which forced them to rewrite. No printing of drafts; we were "green" before our time. And, no student reprinted his draft as his final paper!

When I look back at this assignment, I realize it hit a "sweet spot" in my teaching, as students worked hard and wrote well while getting in touch with their inner selves—their interior landscapes—and found their own path in seeking the universal truths inherent in the questions. While some struggled to grasp the implications of their newfound knowledge, all of them had pushed their own envelopes. I am grateful I asked.

Teaching with wisdom in mind emerges slowly and only when we are open to it. Most likely, it comes to us as much (or more) than our moving towards it. One of my earliest encounters happened in our local cinema with middle schoolers watching Richard Attenborough's *Gandhi*, when I suddenly realized I could change how I approached the world and my classroom. As I observed Ben Kingsley's Gandhi, I understood the power of his presence, and from that moment I began to perceive myself more in who I was and how I behaved rather than what I said. I increasingly observed myself both as a teacher and a person.

Often, wisdom arrives in short phrases. Shunryu Suzuki's, "In the beginner's mind there are many possibilities, but in the expert's there are few"[39] spoke to me. His words were counterintuitive to my drive to be an expert teacher, as I wanted my students and colleagues to know I was well prepared and knowledgeable. I strove to be on top. Suzuki's words taught, however, that I could never complete the expert in me, and also that I needed to remain open to possibilities at every moment. As I became more receptive, I delighted in others' insights, including those of my students and colleagues. Letting go of becoming an expert, I discovered there was less I needed to cling to and more that I could learn.

Later, came Thich Nhat Hanh's "There are two ways to wash the dishes. The first is to wash the dishes in order to have clean dishes and the second is to wash the dishes to wash the dishes."[40] His words opened me to the meaning of being in the moment. My life as a teacher had been an endless chain of completing one task to do the next. "Wash the dishes to wash the dishes" opened the idea of staying present with the task before me. Whenever I stray from this peaceful place, I recall Hanh's words to realign me, often simply by taking a breath. I introduced this idea at a middle school assembly with a talk in which I invited students "to do your homework to do your homework," and paraphrasing Hahn, I added,

> The fact that I am sitting here and doing my homework is a wondrous reality. I am being completely myself, following my breath, conscious of my presence, and conscious of my thoughts and actions. There is no way that I can be tossed around mindlessly, hating what I am doing and wanting to be somewhere else. I am here doing my homework, simply doing my homework. It is a miracle. It's awesome![41]

I put these words on index cards for anyone who wanted one. They disappeared.

As we teach, we develop consistencies. We act as we believe. If we are content driven, we make every effort to portray exciting information to inspire students to want to learn with dynamic, interactive lectures, clever visuals, and intriguing handouts. We believe in our task and strive to realize learning every day. As I reflect on my earlier years, rigor was my top priority, and I required my eighth graders to master the considerable content that was necessary for critical thinking. I also liked to ask provocative questions. Not until I came across Rainer Maria Rilke's famous quotation, however, did I begin to think of balancing the content of my teaching with pursuing inquiry. Rilke wrote,

> [We] should try to love the questions themselves, as if they were locked rooms or books written in a very foreign language . . . Live the questions now. Perhaps then, someday far in the future, you will gradually, without even noticing it, live your way into the answer.[42]

I think I may well have heard these famous words earlier, given their fame, but I was not ready to understand their implications. When we are open to what comes our way, however, we discover new paths, new outlooks, and new investigations. To love the questions meant to become willing to ask before telling, to invite thinking rather than try to fill the mind, and to pursue further questions. To live in the questions meant that I needed to remain patient as students struggled with understanding. My teaching changed—and it evolved.

Had I relied only on exploring the depths of subject matter or the teaching process itself, I may well have missed some of the inner secrets of being a teacher. Certainly, I learned from teachers who were deep into the scholarship and meaning of their subject, but the most intriguing were those who brought "life" into their teaching. I taught better when I was well prepared and best when I was willing to explore implications beyond the material. The deeper my involvement the better my questions, the more interesting the lessons, and the richer the possibilities were for discoveries and insights.

Whenever I had to teach brand new material in which I barely stayed ahead of my students (which can happen to us), I would sometimes feel frustrated. But, when I was willing to stay in the questions and invite my students into the learning process, we had a chance at significant learning. I became more accepting of teaching in this context after a thoughtful conversation with David Spanagel, Assistant Professor at Worcester Polytechnic Institute, when he suggested that sometimes we do our best teaching when we have not yet mastered our subject matter. He may well be right.

This happened when I taught the *Tao Te Ching* as part of an eighth-grade Chinese History course and later an Ancient History course. As I was preparing, my mother happened to give me Benjamin Hoff's *The Tao of Pooh* for Christmas, which became a text along with translations of the *Tao* by Stephen Mitchell. With only a short time to set up the course, my students and I entered the study of the *Tao* together.

By letting go of having to be the expert (again), I could remain open to the wisdom of the *Tao*, not only to reach students but also to learn to teach the *Tao* itself. The result deepened my sense of purpose and direction as a teacher and has stayed with me ever since. In the words of the *Tao*:

If you want to shrink something,
you must first allow it to expand.
If you want to get rid of something,
you must first allow it to flourish.
If you want to take something,
you must first allow it to be given.
This is called the subtle perception
of the way things are.

The soft overcomes the hard.
The slow overcomes the fast.
Let your workings remain a mystery.
Just show people the results.[43]

When my academic-pressured students and I explored the implications that "the soft overcomes the hard," we struggled with it as a counterintuitive message to the drive for excellence. How could we be "soft" in a world defining achievement as success? How could we allow the undesired to flourish when we wanted to get rid of it? While I daresay we lived with more uncertainty than we were used to, we became intrigued with the ambiguity of Taoist thinking. A razor blade, after all, loses its edge from water.

Sometimes, when bringing wisdom into the classroom, I discover some messages were meant for me more than for my students.

Some say that my teaching is nonsense.
Others call it lofty but impractical.
But to those who have looked inside themselves,
this nonsense makes perfect sense.
And to those who put it into practice,
this loftiness has roots that go deep.

I have just three things to teach:
simplicity, patience, compassion.
These three are your greatest treasures.

Simple in actions and in thoughts,
you return to the source of being.
Patient with both friends and enemies,
you accord with the way things are.
Compassionate toward yourself,
you reconcile all beings in the world.[44]

I imagined that if colleagues heard about what transpired in my classroom, they might have considered it nonsense. When teaching an open-education classroom in the 1970s, I became defensive whenever I perceived judgments against what we were trying to accomplish; I once stood on a chair at a faculty meeting and loudly defended our program. But, as I became acquainted with broader perspectives on life and teaching, I became more confident of my approaches and less defensive. Lao Tzu's simplicity, patience, and compassion arrived at the right time. I am still pondering its implications.

Zen stories, Hasidic tales, and Native American wisdom, as well, have fed the soul of my teaching. These came in and out of lessons as needed and created moments of insight for my students and me. Among the most significant was, "The Rabbi's Gift," from Scott Peck, who was not sure of its source. It is the story of a monastery fallen on hard times with only four monks and the abbot. In desperation, the abbot seeks the advice of a rabbi who lived in the nearby woods. After commiserating and reading the Torah together, the rabbi can offer no advice except the mysterious "the Messiah is one of you."

The Abbot returned with the cryptic message, which, in turn, transformed the monastery. The monks, suspecting truth in the rabbi's words, "began to treat each other with extraordinary respect on the chance that one among them might be the Messiah. And they began to treat themselves with extraordinary respect." Soon, more people came to picnic, and young men began to inquire and then joined. "So within a few years the monastery had once again become a thriving order, and thanks to the rabbi's gift, a vibrant center of light and spirituality in the realm."[45]

I found a deep knowing in this story. How amazing to imagine each student as the Messiah, and how much more of a challenge to think of my colleagues—or me!—as the Messiah. The rabbi's gift to the abbot encouraged me once again to let go of assumptions about others, to see the gifts in everyone (including myself), and to live in the present. While I may not have always succeeded, the gift of this story assures me that I will always try. I imagine classrooms where teachers and students "treat each other with extraordinary respect" and "treat themselves with extraordinary respect." What a difference that would make!

As I write, I recall more and more of these magical moments from the wisdom that continues to feed my teaching. I've discovered these truths sometimes when I allow stillness to be present. As the *Tao* says, "We join spokes together in a wheel, /but it is the center hole /that makes the wagon move."[46] I can't imagine teaching without such sources. Given the enormous responsibility we have to reach the young and engage them, we need all the help we can find.

"God blooms from the shoulder of the Elephant who becomes courteous to the Ant."[47] Hafiz says it all.

REFLECTION

Paying attention to the wisdom that guides our lives enriches our teaching. When we invite our accumulated wisdom into our teaching, we deepen our commitment to and understanding about why we chose to teach. We allow our real selves to enter the classroom and to become receptive to the lives and spirit of our students. If, on the other hand, we deny the presence of our deeper selves, we deny the opportunity to see the deeper selves of our students.

Dan Hilliard grew up in a socially religious home; his family joined a church when he was twelve years old. In his early years teaching, he had little time to find a church, but after attending David Mallery's conference at Westtown, a Quaker School, he discovered he liked the contemplativeness of Quaker Meeting and decided to attend. Since then he has learned about eastern philosophy, astrology, past-life regression, and other alternative spiritual philosophies. He decided some years ago to fit in "alternative" ideas whenever possible in his teaching. He believes not only should his students be exposed to mainstream thinking, but also to other ways to open their minds and raise questions.

POINTS TO PURSUE

☑ What seminal poem, book, reading, essay, or film feeds your teaching? How does it speak to your teaching? Have you shared it with your students? With your colleagues?

☑ What is the "deepest" assignment you ever gave? Did it push the envelope of your students' minds? What unexpected results did it bring to them? To you? Were you ready for what happened?

☑ How can we bring questions into the heart of our teaching, especially given our perceived need to teach quickly? How can we in the words of Rilke, "love the questions themselves," and take time in our classrooms to "live in the questions now," and trust that together we'll "live [our] way into the answer?" How can we not choose to teach in this way at a time when we live with a predictably uncertain future?

☑ What allows us to risk teaching a subject with which we are not familiar? How can we sometimes let go of thinking we have to be the expert, then delve into unfamiliar territory, trusting that we can learn it alongside our students? Can we invite them to openly explore with us?

☑ What if we took "The Rabbi's Gift" to heart and saw every student, every parent, every colleague, our principal—and possibly ourselves—as the Messiah? What difference would it make?

CHAPTER 9

Stay Current

I have struggled to understand why change in schools is so difficult. We come into contact with compelling ideas, ones we swear we'd like to adopt, but soon we find ourselves maintaining habitual behaviors. This happened to me after seeing Frederick Wiseman's documentary *Meat* in the mid-seventies.[48] As Wiseman took viewers from the stockyard to the supermarket meat counter, I became convinced never to eat meat again. My resolve lasted about two weeks, maybe three. I still can recall Wiseman's disturbing black-and-white images but I continue to enjoy my chicken and beef.

Recently, I read Jonathan Haidt's remarkable concept of the rider (mind) and the elephant (body) in his book *The Happiness Hypothesis*.[49] The elephant in us enacts habitual practices we've learned that sustain our daily lives, what we do automatically. The rider, on the other hand, represents our minds looking ahead and around, wondering, speculating, and conjuring alternatives. The rider is the viewer of Wiseman's documentary who commits to becoming a vegetarian. She is the teacher who attends a statewide workshop on brain research, brings back new ideas for revamping lessons, and shares her excitement with colleagues; yet, three weeks later, she is practicing as she always has, the ideas from the workshop having receded into the background.

Why does this happen? Haidt's rider and elephant metaphor can help us. Sometimes, we make radical changes in our lives on our own—changes that retrain our elephant. Some quit smoking one day never to smoke again. Others quit sweets and desserts to maintain low blood sugar. And some commit to exercise for health and fitness and stick to it. Still, as this book makes clear, change in teaching has been slow, as the continued persistence of teaching from the front of the room testifies.

Perhaps it's because we teach alone. To make changes, we need support and encouragement from people close to us, but teachers next door to us teach alone, too. Even when we try something different, we do not feel we have enough time, as we need to maintain the regular coverage curriculum to meet external demands. Sometimes, students have difficulty adapting to a new approach, so we back off and pledge, perhaps, to try it again next year. It's easier and less stressful to let the elephant continue to do its thing. Besides, we have little incentive to change, and no one to hold us accountable.

As I reexamined my thinking about staying current when rewriting this chapter, I imagined facing a new group of eighth graders on the first day of school in 2010, more than ten years after my last year in the classroom. As I describe in Chapter 5, "Rearrange Rooms," I used to intrigue my students at the end of the first day in class by sending them home with Carl Duncker's monk on the mountain problem (made famous by Arthur Koestler).[50] It had become a staple for opening the year, part of the elephant of my teaching. I sent students home knowing this simply stated problem, replete with extraneous information, would generate discussion at the dinner table even in busy households.

The problem, as expected, baffled most of my students and their families, thus reinforcing my resolve to explore problems and issues requiring perseverance. Learning in my classroom was, first and foremost, about creative and critical thinking, finding meaning, and solving mysteries.

If I were still in the classroom today and wanted to keep a similar focus, I could not successfully begin the year with this problem, presented in the same way. Why? Google, of course! My students would simply search "koestler monk on the mountain" and the first result would be the problem and the solution. They would have no motivation—or need—to figure it out on their own.

Before Google ("BG"), teachers had the freedom to intrigue, to surprise, and often to be the first to bring new ideas to students. Early in my teaching, I could count on being able to expose my students to something new and take time to explore its implications. As the years passed, I observed students knowing more and more, until in my later years, I rarely was able to surprise them. Now, I imagine it's impossible. After Google ("AG"), anyone can find almost anything, immediately—and information finds us! It seems people are satisfied if and when they can have information quickly. Why bother to make the effort to figure anything out?

So, to teach my eighth graders in 2010—or 12 AG[51]—how can

I continue to intrigue my students with the monk on the mountain? How can I prevent access to Google from short-circuiting their thinking? Here's a possible scenario:

1. When students arrive, have them check their cell phones and BlackBerries at the door (if they have them). Explain why and briefly tell them what to expect.
2. Begin the class with the monk on the mountain problem. Invite them to solve it (alone or with others) using paper and pencil or the whiteboard.
3. Challenge them to solve it during class, and ask them to demonstrate their solution, if they can. If some solve it quickly (or if they already know it), ask them to observe others and prepare to share their observations about how their classmates approached the problem.
4. If no one solves it, try to tease a solution or two from the class.
5. Invite students to take the problem home and share it, then bring back the result the next day. Encourage them not to look it up on Google—a real test of self-control!

Staying current means in part to acknowledge the contexts within which we teach and respond in ways to stimulate creative and critical thinking. In the Google Age, we need to separate creativity and thinking from Googling information, if we intend our students to become lifelong learners equipped to teach themselves. They need to learn that Google knowledge should serve to support thinking and creating, but not act as a substitute. Given the glitter and ease of use of Google, Twitter, and texting, students will avoid wrestling with challenging and difficult problems, let alone have the time to do so.

Which brings us to the question of providing students with laptops in the classroom. When I first learned that the state of Maine decided to provide them to all seventh graders, I was encouraged. Here was a state willing to commit to bringing schools into the new age of technology. Since then, however, I have had second thoughts. I began to imagine students in my classroom focused on their laptops taking notes, fact checking my teaching, and chatting with friends. Opportunities for face-to-face interactions would decrease. There would be no more threaded conversations in which we look and listen to one another, observe facial expressions, and attend to intonations. Instead, my students would be tethered to their flat screens, engaging and disengaging their minds from the intended learning, never becoming a community of learners. If we were to lose the ability to interact together face-to-face, it would be like losing a language—a fundamental human language at that!

Bud Brooks, Director of Institutional Technology at Bancroft School in Worcester, Massachusetts, suggests that instead of laptops in the classroom, we allow cell phones with access to Web 2.0.[52] Teachers and students could take advantage of the potential of communication, information sharing, interoperability, and collaboration, as they access the Web within the context of their learning. Most of the time—at least in my classroom, I'd imagine—we would be face-to-face, and we would use the phones when we sensed the need.

As the rider, we need to shift how we think about teaching in order to engage the brains of today's learners. We need to retrain our teaching habits and approaches—our elephant—to make learning more possible. Sometimes, it may mean separating the young from their electronic devices to challenge their minds to think, create, and resolve. Other times, it may mean integrating these devices into the classroom. We need to know when and how.

Since the 1990s, we have learned more about the brain than during all prior years combined. MRIs, fMRIs, and Pet Scans allow us to observe the brain at work and continue to teach us about this miraculous organ. As educators, we cannot ignore the implications of this research, but we must apply it cautiously in order to teach more effectively. The following are some brain-research-derived concepts with significant implications for teaching and learning:

- Mihaly Csikszentmihalyi's Flow
- Howard Gardner's Multiple Intelligences
- The difference between short-term and long-term memory learning

- Down-shifting (shutting down emotionally) limits thinking under stress.

- Eustress (positive stress; just enough to stimulate) differs from distress.

- When people talk they learn.

- The brain's natural inclination is to seek patterns.

- Feedback plays an essential role in learning.

- Exercise is crucial to stimulate learning.

A radical idea from brain research that I explore with teachers to demonstrate its importance comes from David Sousa's *Primacy-Recency* (Figure 9.1).[53] Essentially, it advocates teaching in response to how the brain learns best by placing the major input portion of our lessons at the front of a learning episode; then providing time to process during the middle; and concluding with active summarizers to cement the learning. Teachers acknowledge, however, that they concentrate their teaching during the middle of the period, after collecting homework, taking attendance, giving announcements, and handling other non-instructional matters; they conclude by giving students time to begin homework or to relax until the bell. The curved line I've added to Figure 9.1 represents this. After all, this is the way most of us learned in school.

Once a teacher told me she tried to realign her teaching by applying the Primacy-Recency principle, but discovered that her students were unable to adjust. She decided to quit trying but promised she would try again at the beginning of the next year; whether she did or not, I do not know. I have known only two other teachers who have made an effort to implement it.

Where, then, does this leave us? First, the primary challenge facing us is to recognize that we must make changes in our practice. Second, we have to pay attention to new content, ideas, and approaches and decide which ones are necessary and essential to adopt. Third—the most difficult and most important—we have to commit and follow

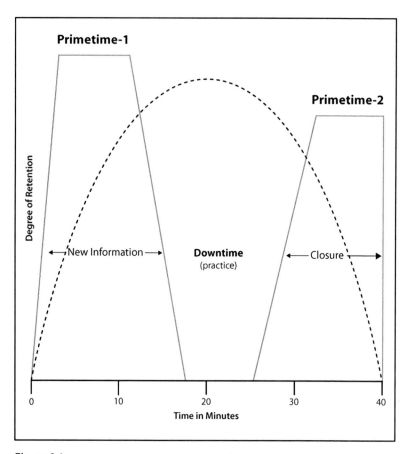

Figure 9.1.

Primacy-Recency—Retention During a Learning Episode.

(Adapted from David Sousa, *How the Brain Learns: A Classroom Teacher's Guide.* Revised Edition. [Thousand Oaks, CA: Corwin Press, 2001], 90. Used by permission of the publisher.)

through to integrate these changes into our teaching. Walk the talk. Engage the elephant.

We can begin by committing to stay current with educational research and literature, as well as works by authors outside the field who speak to our efforts. Teachers still argue that because of the daily demands of multiple commitments, inside and outside of school, they do not have time.

The *Marshall Memo*, which debuted in August 2003, is the perfect tool to support the habit of staying current.[54] Publisher and educator Kim Marshall serves as a "designated teacher's reader" who subscribes to forty-four publications and gleans from them important and relevant articles for teachers and administrators. He writes cogent synopses that he emails to subscribers on Monday evenings.

Whenever I share the *Marshall Memo*, the rider in teachers, as well as administrators, responds enthusiastically. But when I follow up weeks later, few, if any, teachers have subscribed; administrators, on the other hand, are more likely to sign up. This is, perhaps, because they have discretionary funds for such purposes.

Here are some strong first steps for staying current:

- Explore Kim Marshall's Website, http://www.marshallmemo .com, download and read the sample *Marshall Memo*, then invite colleagues and the administration to do the same and discuss signing up.

- Ask the administration if they would be willing to provide subscriptions for the faculty. This drops the cost precipitously. If they do not agree, gather as many teachers as possible to subscribe as a group to lower the cost.

- Once you have subscribed, commit to reading the *Marshall Memo* every week at the same time; it will take less than a half-hour. You can do this alone or even better, read it with colleagues either in school or after. You could establish a "*Marshall Memo* Club," in which you could report on ideas you have tried from the *Marshall Memo*.

- Encourage the principal to use *Marshall Memo* articles at faculty meetings. It would not only motivate faculty and staff to read them, but it would also encourage active participation to foster collegiality around important ideas and practices. Presenting the *Marshall Memo* at faculty meetings nurtures the habit of reading it, and more importantly, integrates the latest and best thinking throughout the school's culture.

- Take advantage of articles from the *Marshall Memo* for team and department meetings. Team heads or department chairs could access its database for relevant articles to put on the agenda; if several articles apply, the teachers could jigsaw to encourage articulating and sharing.

If we adopt ideas such as these, we would have multiple reasons for subscribing. Instead of being left alone to read and attempt new ideas in isolation (an unrealistic expectation), we would begin to develop collegial relationships and feel support to examine new and different practices. The *Marshall Memo* would likely become part of our practice—and help us retrain our elephant.

While the *Marshall Memo* provides access to the latest thinking and research, we also need to take time to dig deeper. By subscribing to *The Main Idea*,[55] which offers elegant eight-page summaries (not reviews) of eight to ten current educational books a year, we can explore some topics more in depth. Jenn David-Lang, founder and scribe, captures the big ideas in a readable and useful format. Norman Atkins, CEO Uncommon Schools and Co-Founder, North Star Academy Charter School writes on *The Main Idea*'s Website that "[Jenn] has the heart of a teacher, the brain of a think tank, and the patience of a librarian."

Among the notable books David-Lang has summarized are Richard Dufour, et al., *Learning by Doing*; Heidi Hayes Jacobs, *Active Literacy Across the Curriculum*; Richard Stiggins, et al., *Classroom Assessment for Student Learning*; John Saphier, et al., *The Skillful Teacher*; and Ross Greene's, *Lost at School: Why Our Kids with Behavioral Challenges are Falling Through the Cracks and How We Can Help Them*.[56]

David-Lang also designs workshops for subscribers. For example, she put together a classroom management workshop with handouts based on Harry K. and Rosemary T. Wong, *The First Days of School*,[57] which she also summarized. As with the *Marshall Memo*, teachers could form *The Main Idea* book groups to encourage self-directed professional development.

Some schools make it a practice to purchase books for faculty to encourage professional reading and stimulate discussions and new thinking. It is important, however, that we participate in selecting books and facilitating discussions, otherwise we might resent being told to do one more thing.

Staying current with the latest research and methodologies is not optional. We, like all professionals, need to align ourselves to best practices. Not to do so deprives our students of what they deserve. Global demands, technologies, and media are forcing us to reassess our practices. Paying attention to new knowledge, understandings, and pedagogies will keep us relevant and essential in educating the young. This book invites the rider in us to look ahead and around at significant ideas and practices that we can adopt to retrain our elephant to teach effectively from the middle of the room.

REFLECTION

When Dan Hilliard first learned about the rider and the elephant metaphor from a colleague, he began to understand why he had been having difficulty changing his deep-seated practices. He'd already given up New Year's resolutions, since they never materialized. He started reflecting on his teaching practices and realized he did many of them without thinking. For example, collecting homework at the beginning of class; passing out quizzes, tests, and papers during class; sometimes taking excessive time on non-instructional matters; often calling on the first hands raised; and keeping his students' desks in rows.

He wondered how he could better inform his rider, so he could consider other options to begin retraining his elephant. He decided to ask colleagues if he could observe them during his planning periods. Perhaps he would discover better ways to interact with his students. He also heard about a school in the next town renowned for its alternative approaches to teaching and learning. He decided to ask his principal if he could go visit and come back and report to the rest of the faculty. He also asked if the school could subscribe to the *Marshall Memo* and *The Main Idea*.

POINTS TO PURSUE

☑ Make a list of common practices you use in your classroom. Indicate on a scale from 1 to 4 the effectiveness of these practices. Try to eliminate your less effective practices and explore alternatives. Show your list to colleagues to seek their input—and to encourage them to do the same.

☑ Consider the rider and the elephant in your teaching. How often has your rider wanted to try something new, but soon the idea slipped away? How difficult has it been to take on new ideas and practices in your classroom? Can you find ways to connect with colleagues when implementing a new practice? When have you been able to successfully retrain your elephant? Under what conditions?

☑ Commit to implementing a new practice you value (such as, Primacy-Recency) and stick to it no matter how difficult. If need be, do it quietly, without fanfare, to see what happens. If it fails, give yourself credit for your efforts—and try another!

☑ Explore the *Marshall Memo* as explained in this chapter and take it as far as you can into your school culture. Having a clear end in mind will encourage you to persist.

☑ Subscribe to Jenn David-Lang's *The Main Idea* to develop the habit of paying attention to new and significant literature in the field.

☑ Form a teachers' book club with interested colleagues. Commit to reading books from inside and outside the field.

CHAPTER 10

Seek the Higher Road

When I stepped into my first classroom more than forty years ago, I found the desks and chairs in rows, much as Dan Hilliard did, facing the teacher's desk and a blackboard. It was true in every room. It had been the same when, as pupils, we sat in chairs at desks looking at our teachers. Even now, when we walk through corridors, we still see most teachers up front talking as we did and as our teachers did, an image imprinted onto readers of this book.

Let's reopen our conversation:

Why have we insisted on maintaining our grip on teaching from the front of the room?

Why do we continue to choose to talk more than we listen?

Why do we still believe giving information is more important than processing it?

Why do we persist in teaching the same material to all students at the same time?

What prevents us from taking the higher road of creative, challenging, interactive, and provocative teaching?

Perhaps, it's because we work in a profession that prides itself on consistency. I imagine some of us believe that our traditions are anchors in the storm of change. Such consistency, however, often does more to serve our needs and less to meet the multiple worlds of our digitally-wired students. We see them as unable to stay on task during our lessons; they see us as taking too long to make our point.

Still, we view our responsibility as information bearers. We establish authority from the front by directing our students' eyes towards us. Beginning in first grade, they see us taking charge. They learn to do school well, and by the time they reach middle and high school, they know the drill. It becomes second nature. It is still second nature when we decide to become teachers and take our turn at the front.

Unlike professionals in medicine, law, and business, we enter teaching already knowing (or thinking we know) how to teach, as we have been observing teachers since kindergarten. While other professions require internships, residencies, and apprenticeships, we student teach for a brief time and then become full-fledged teachers on the first day in our classrooms. From that day on, most of us teach alone—and receive little or no feedback. We have little impetus to change.

We also hesitate to change because of increasing pressures from federal and state governments that demand adequate yearly progress on tests scores. We are required to cover more and more material to meet this demand—and to do it faster. So, we find it easier to stick with methods we know—and tell students what we want them to know.

But we are reaching fewer students. And more of them are on independent educational plans (IEPs), as society identifies more disabilities that require special education. In efforts to create equity and equal opportunity for each student, we establish more inclusion classes to mainstream the learning disabled. Yet, we persist using old methods and hope somehow all will learn. We do what we know.

In the end, perhaps it's simply easier to stay at the front. Perhaps we do what we know because it creates less stress and more peace of mind as we confront the multiple complexities of everyday teaching. At least it seems that way.

Perhaps it's easier:

- To tell students what to learn rather than to take time to empower them to participate in designing their learning

- To call on the first hands raised, repeat the answer, and then elaborate to complete the lesson rather than to engage students in serious dialogue in which we partner in their learning

- To give true-false, short-answer, multiple-choice tests (particularly ones written by publishers) rather than to design authentic performance assessments

- To teach from textbooks rather than to take time to design and implement innovative programs using the textbook as a resource

- To teach all the kids the same material at the same time rather than to provide relevant materials based on student readiness, interest, or learning style
- To teach in our preferred style rather than to adjust to the different learning styles of our students
- To teach lessons from old notes that we ask students to copy, year after year, and give the same quizzes and tests rather than to rework, redesign, and make relevant what we want students to know, understand, and be able to do
- To assign reading and writing as homework rather than to teach these literacy skills in class
- To give the same homework assignments rather than to provide choice, alternatives, or to let students create their own
- To leave at the close of school and take care of personal business rather than to stay after school to collaborate with colleagues
- To watch a favorite television show at the end of the day rather than to read a journal or professional book; after all, we are tired.

The veterans among us will recognize that these "easier" ways describe how we were taught to teach. We learned to focus on whole-class lessons in which the "smartest" students received As, and the "less able" received lower grades. We decided what to deliver without much concern or interest in what colleagues taught. We acted as independent agents, free to pursue teaching as it suited us.

But now we know differently. Even those among us who still practice "easier" ways, know that they are no longer adequate. We know that students differ in how they learn. We know that incessant lectures put their minds to sleep. We know that they do not like homework as much as we believed they used to. We know that what we used to do—and believe we did well—is no longer enough, because, we know that they learn best from invoking their interests and building on what they know.

We know that choosing to teach unconventionally will take courage and relentless effort. Doing it the "easier" way has allowed us to become comfortable, as we teach like everyone else does: not rocking the boat; keeping students and parents quiet and happy (or seemingly happy); and being safe, right, and normal. When we decide to teach differently, it means to take on the role of the underdog—to become Davids in a world of Goliaths.[58] It means deciding, on our own if we must, what we need to do to make sensible learning happen. It means giving up and letting go of practices that no longer work. It means hard work, tireless effort, and persistence, persistence, persistence—nothing less.

If we choose to continue down the "easier" path, more of our students will not learn. We only fool ourselves if we believe that we are teaching well because some students are willing to sit and listen, take notes, study, and ace our tests; if the other students tried harder they, too, would get good grades. We look back and remember how few of *our* classmates earned As, yet most of them found ways to succeed in the world.

We can't afford to teach this way any more. We need to take a higher road, and pay attention to colleagues who have chosen this road, colleagues who:

- Hold high expectations for all students—and succeed beyond all expectations

- Challenge all students, acknowledge their different learning styles, and make sure each one learns before moving on

- Persist in taking risks to find better ways for students to learn

- Create or join study groups to examine best practices, lessons, and student work

- Take time to create feedback opportunities through mutual observations and conferencing

- Meet regularly with colleagues using agendas designed to improve instruction

- Mentor and nurture new colleagues offering support, ideas, and compassion

- Stay after school to prepare and meet with colleagues

- Go the extra mile for students every day and on weekends
- Attend students' games and performances after school

Every school district has pockets of "Davids" who have abandoned the "easier" path and have responded to the challenges schools and families are facing. These are the great teachers among us. We all know who they are. They have taken the higher road. They've signed the Teaching Manifesto.[59]

REFLECTION

Dan Hilliard sometimes cringes at the criticism of his fellow teachers. Yes, they stay at the front of the room most of the time, but they are not necessarily poor teachers. His colleague, Josh Wilson, enthralls his students by sharing his stories and insights into the novels he teaches. He talks much of the time, but his students can't wait for his next class. But, Dan realizes too many teachers treat teaching as telling, and fail to intrigue their students. He wishes he could share his own ideas on this subject but finds it difficult. Few teachers appear open to publicly assessing their teaching. It's just not done.

POINTS TO PURSUE

☑ Undoubtedly, all fields have practitioners who prefer "the old ways" rather than move forward in response to newfound needs of constituents. Teachers are infamous for such behavior. The story of Rip Van Winkle awakening one hundred years later finding an unrecognizable world except for the classroom has more truth than we'd like to admit. Have you wondered why so many of us persist in teaching as our teachers taught us and their teachers taught them? What parts of that teacher should you treasure? What parts should you let go?

☑ Given our historic role as information bearers, how has the Internet affected what we share? What information should we convey to our students? What information should we discover together? What information do they need know (other than what they can find by "Googling it")?

☑   What allows us to continue to practice the "easier" methods described above? Perhaps it's because no one is watching or observing us. What will drive us to change? (Certainly, we will not be paid more if we do.)

☑   Taking the higher road enacts our true calling. If we've hesitated to commit ourselves to this level, what is holding us back? We see others bubbling with enthusiasm and love for their work. In tough circumstances, they seem to find the silver linings and move forward. Nothing gets in the way of what they want to accomplish. If you want to deepen your commitment, don't hesitate to ask one of these teachers for help. They will be honored.

☑   Are you a "David" among your colleagues? Or do you know other teachers who are? How do you/they persist, despite the conventional teaching surrounding you/them? What keeps the "Davids" from succumbing to the "Goliaths?"

PART III

What Must We Change?

Education, like other institutions, has embedded practices that obstruct sensible, relevant, and productive teaching. Most of these practices originate from previous paradigms. The most insidious originated from factory-model schools designed to meet the demands of the industrial era. These hierarchically structured monoliths were led by managers (men) hiring cheap labor (women) to carry out scripted lessons to groups of children who were sorted out by IQ. This structure still prevails, despite the pressures and demands of a rapidly changing culture and impact of the global world.

The isolated classroom teacher remains as the unfortunate legacy of this paradigm. Despite major efforts across the country to implement standards and unify curriculums within districts, most of us continue to teach much as we always have—and more so in response to the demands of high-stakes tests.

If we intend to uproot ineffective embedded traditions, we have to adopt the-emperor-is-not-wearing-any-clothes attitude. We need to pay attention to the effects of those practices—those caused by others *and* by us—that interfere with reaching the potential of each and every student, namely: tracking, unions, interruptions, and the persistence of whole class lessons. We need to pay attention to how they interfere with reaching our own potential. Together, reforming these practices will free our students and us to become people able to live the lives we deserve, to gain the freedom we crave, and to find the happiness we desire.

CHAPTER 11

Abolish Tracking

"Who's not going to get it?"
"Who will already know it or get it quickly?"

The habit of preparing one lesson for the whole class resides deep in the DNA of teaching. But, when I ask the above two questions, teachers in my workshops immediately bring students to mind. The door swings open to alternative approaches to lessons.

I show videos of two teachers who adjust their teaching to meet different levels of understanding.[60] In the first video, a science teacher assigns three groups of students to investigate a concept. She assigns her middle group to an at-grade-level lab activity usually done with the whole class; she decides to give an advanced group a simulation designed to stretch their thinking; and she provides her struggling learners a computer to assist in handling data.[61] In the second video, a math teacher assigns three groups of sixth graders to work on the same math concept: One group uses manipulatives, and the other two groups use textbooks, one book at grade level and the other more advanced.

I point out that these teachers' desire to make learning accessible for every student is like what coaches do when responding to players' skill levels. My workshop participants usually do not question this analogy. After some conversation, however, someone inevitably suggests that the groupings represent either a hidden form of tracking or a type of ability grouping. Some imagine these students remaining in the same groups, despite the video's claim they've been put in "readiness" groups for that lesson based on their demonstrated level of understanding of the material. Others say the teachers in the video should not have allowed students to work at different levels, because some would be stigmatized while others rewarded.

But, when I show a third video, the conversation becomes heated.[62] In it, a fourth-grade teacher demonstrates incorporating student interest by allowing her students to study an historical figure of their choice. After dividing students into three groups based on their choices, she provides multiple levels of books from which they can choose. The first part of the video, shows students studying a person of their choice and reading books at their comfort levels.

The next part, however, challenges viewers' perceptions of fair classroom teaching. The teacher passes out three different colored cubes (red, green, and blue) to individual students sitting at their respective tables. She asks all of them to use the "compare and contrast" side on each cube: Those having red cubes are to draw a picture of their historical person and a member of their family and write a comparison; those with green are to use a Venn diagram; and those with blue are to create an open-ended compare-and-contrast diagram. The teacher has no qualms about using colored cubes, nor apparently do her students.

But my teachers often do. "I can't abide having students know that some are 'better' than others," someone invariably states. "It's not right to group kids like that," another adds. "How do you think the 'red-group kids' feel seeing their classmates doing higher-level work?" "It's not fair to allow some kids to do higher-level work in front of their peers." The outrage continues. Sometimes, I'm able to reframe the issue from a broader perspective and sometimes not.

Paradoxically, participants criticize the video teachers, on the one hand, for setting up "readiness" groups for lessons as a form of tracking, and on the other, validate their own school's decision to make permanent homogeneous groupings for "bright," "average," and "slow" students. Such descriptors dominate nearly all conversations about students. By the end of the discussion, the video teachers' message often becomes lost as teachers defend their groupings. Pressures to perform well on state and federal assessment, they argue, demands they teach as fast as possible and in the way they know best: Making "readiness" groups would take too much time; "ability" groups are more efficient.

We circle back to the fundamental question, "Why do we insist on teaching using the same assumptions and methods our teachers used?" Has it crept into our DNA? Perhaps terms, such as "bright," "average," and "slow" are embedded in the language of the profession. I remember struggling to avoid thinking in those terms early in my career. The longer I taught the more students surprised me when their abilities surfaced. I do not remember when I fully realized that my perception of students as "slow" might be due to their self-identification as "slow" as a strategy to protect themselves from being discovered as not smart. Nevertheless, I often found myself prejudging when I should have waited.

I was fortunate early in my career to have a student who was willing to speak her mind. After telling me how much she enjoyed my class several years before, Hillary added, "One thing, Mr. Thoms, that bothered me then was you seemed to decide early which students were smarter and which were not, and you never changed your mind." I was stunned. From that day, I vowed to stay open to the potential of each student—and to every teacher I teach. I have to catch myself at times, but I keep at it, asking myself these questions:

Do we hear what we actually say when we are discussing students and grouping?

Do we really think some students are "bright" and others "slow"?

Do we really believe we can achieve more with our "bright" groups than we can with our "slower" groups?

Do we prefer "bright" (cooperative) kids who play the game of school well and are "easier" to teach?

Do we assume the "lower groups" (uncooperative) are less teachable?

Do we really think we no longer track students as we were tracked?

Even after viewing clips of *Stand and Deliver*, in which Jamie Escalante demonstrates the effectiveness of holding high expectations for all of his students, I hear teachers use this language of tracking as if it is etched in their minds. I think I understand why it persists. Teachers, after all, deal with large numbers of students, often well over one hundred per day in middle and high school, so an expedient terminology is useful. Also, because they have to sort and grade students, these categories facilitate that process. And, labeling is endemic in our culture.

The real danger in using this terminology is its threat to student potential. It's one matter to see them as struggling or behind in their efforts to learn at a given moment, since this information helps us find ways to help them progress to the next level. It's another to determine they are "slow" or at "level one" because they have done poorly in academics. Once we categorize them, their fate in school has been sealed. We no longer seek their potential. They no longer believe in themselves.

But, we can shift our thinking to become open to surprise, to the "Aha! moments" that signal a sudden grasp of a concept, an understanding, or an insight. We can teach by invoking the mantra, "Expect the surprise and it will come." We can acknowledge that the habit of sorting resides in all of us, as it was the foundation of the factory-based public schools system we know well. But when we become aware of the harm of sorting, we open to every student's potential. Having surprise in our mind alerts us to the possible, away from the numbness of prejudgment.

How can we break out of this predicament? We can begin by realizing students do not have a fixed intelligence, as we examined in Chapter 7, "See the Big Picture." IQ can be influential for entering a field of study or career but has little to do with determining success.[63] Also, the ability to delay gratification is a better predictor than one's intelligence level in determining successful academic performance.[64] Once we have these understandings, we can let go of labeling students as "slow" or "bright," focus on high expectations for all, and nurture each student's potential. We all know of teachers like:

- Jaime Escalante, whose East Los Angeles Hispanic students all passed the AP Calculus exam.[65]

- Marva Collins, whose Chicago elementary student on *60 Minutes* responded to Morley Safer's hard question about his school: "Why do you like it? It's just too hard," to which the boy replied, "That's why I like it, because it makes your brain bigger."[66]

- Rafe Esquith whose Los Angeles ELA fifth graders read, among other books, *Of Mice and Men*, *The Joy Luck Club*, and *To Kill a Mockingbird*—and produce a full-length Shakespearean play every year.[67]

We need to see these teachers not as exceptional but as illustrative of what all of us can do. When we choose to set teachers aside as special or exceptional, we excuse ourselves from becoming like them. Instead, they represent values we all need to strive for:

- Holding high expectations for all students
- Believing in every student regardless of perceived abilities
- Asking the most from students every day, every class
- Nurturing each student along the way
- Becoming learners fascinated with learning

Or, in their own words:

- Jaime Escalante: "You're going to work harder than you ever have before. The only thing I ask from you is "ganas" (desire). If you don't have "ganas," I will give it to you, because I am an expert."[68]
- Marva Collins: "There's no magic here. Mrs. Collins is no miracle worker. I do not walk on water; I do not part the sea. I just love children and work harder than a lot of people, and so will you."[69]
- Rafe Esquith: "There are no shortcuts."[70]

Those of us who see students as fixed quantities, such as "bright" or "slow," can choose to break away from this mindset by remembering our teachers who may have judged us unfairly. Some of us may still have residual feelings, but have managed to make our lives work, though not without struggle. Hopefully, we will not create such a burden on our students.

Perhaps we carry these judgments into the classroom. Perhaps we still see ourselves as average in a career that is low on the social ladder, and less respected than other professions. Regardless of our origins, we need not replicate what happened to us. We need not continue to label as we were labeled.

We must find our own path to greatness if we are to create these paths for our students, and heed the wisdom of Marianne Williamson (erroneously attributed to Nelson Mandela who quoted it at his inaugural):

Our deepest fear is not that we are inadequate. Our deepest fear is that we are powerful beyond measure. It is our light, not our darkness, that most frightens us. We ask ourselves, who am I to be brilliant, gorgeous, talented, fabulous? Actually who are you not to be? You are a child of God. Your playing small does not serve the world. There's nothing enlightened about shrinking so that other people won't feel insecure around you. We are all meant to shine as children do. We were born to make manifest the glory of God within us; it's in everyone. And as we let our light shine, we unconsciously give other people permission to do the same. As we're liberated from our own fear, our presence automatically liberates others.[71]

Jamie Escalante, Marva Collins, and Rafe Esquith and the great teachers we've known do not "do small." Why should we?

The seminal work of Carol Dweck provides insight both for understanding ourselves and understanding how we perceive our students. In *Mindset: The New Psychology of Success*,[72] she describes two possible mindsets people have: a *fixed* mindset or a *growth* mindset. People who have a *fixed* mindset believe their abilities, personality, and moral character are fixed, and their responses to circumstances either prove or disprove their worth. People who have a *growth* mindset, on the contrary, believe their initial talents, interests, aptitudes, and temperaments can be changed through effort. Every challenge becomes an opportunity.

Simply recognizing these two paths can have a profound impact on our teaching. If we stop to think how much we rely on test scores, judgments of previous teachers, class placements, and our own initial impressions to determine the abilities of our students, we might realize we do not have a clue—not a clue!—about their true potential. As Dweck reminds us, were we to have been Mozart's teacher in the first ten years of his writing music, we might have written him off as mediocre. Were we to have been Edison's teacher in his early years, we would not have recognized his entrepreneurial skills.

From the moment we understand our teaching is all about growth and not about reward, we can make the following commitment:

I will not judge any student's potential by what he has done in the past or what he has done today. Instead, I will accept what we are not good at as challenges and opportunities for making our brains bigger—my students' and mine!

We might put this commitment on our refrigerator.

We become advocates, then, against placing students based on IQ or single-placement tests. We know some of them learn at a higher level but not always for reasons related to intelligence. While we support advanced-level courses for those who have learned the prerequisites, we cannot deny equal opportunities to others. We will remind our colleagues that less capable students and athletes can (and do) outperform their talented counterparts. We will also remind them of the crucial role of teachers and coaches. Ask any successful coach why good teams thrive with players of mixed abilities. The research also shows that mixed-ability classes are beneficial for all learners.[73] And, as Richard Lavoie points, out regular students always benefit from being in inclusion classes.[74]

Janice, a participant in one of my workshops, recounted an instance in her graduate class when she had forgotten to put her name on a paper. When the professor asked two of his best students if the "A" paper belonged to one of them, his jaw dropped when he saw it was hers. She realized not only that he had assumed she was probably incapable of such a paper but also how badly this made her feel— *and*, more importantly, she recognized how she and her colleagues assumed, as did her professor, that some of *their* students were less capable.

Other times, labeling creates tragedies. In one instance, an elementary special education teacher assigned her students reading books, which they enjoyed. After several weeks, however, the supervising teacher discovered that she had given them "advanced" books by mistake and immediately replaced them with "more appropriate" materials. This incident reminded me of an episode of *The Simpsons* in which Bart was placed in a remedial class and wondered how working slower would help him catch up to the other kids.

One more example: I overheard Jessica, a ninth-grade history teacher, say in a loud voice to her colleagues after a workshop, "I don't know if I could teach this concept to my 'lower-level' kids." No one challenged her assumption and instead nodded in agreement. I was struck by the finality of her statement and how unaware she and her colleagues were of the implications of what she had said. They all believed her "top" classes would be able to discuss and debate while her "lower" classes could not. How sad.

Such comments recall Jerome Bruner's famous declaration, "We begin with the hypothesis that any subject can be taught effectively in some intellectually honest form to any child at any stage of development."[75] Few disagree with Bruner when they take time to think about it, yet teachers and schools largely ignore it. What if, instead, we took Bruner's words to heart and used them as a mantra, as Tom Vreeland, a volunteer tutor who had unwavering optimism about students' potential to learn, did when tutoring students who twice had failed to pass the Massachusetts high-stakes test.[76]

When I see teachers who appear willing to give up on students, I sometimes share the story of Robert Golomb from Malcolm Gladwell's book, *Blink: The Power of Thinking Without Thinking*. Golomb, a virtuoso car salesman, has an exceptional intelligence for dealing with people. His resolve to take care of every customer who comes through the door prevents him from prejudging. As a result, he remains open to every potential buyer, unlike his colleagues who pre-assess customers' looks—factoring in (unconsciously perhaps) their age, race, and gender—not only to decide how to treat them but also to gauge their inclination to buy. But, because Golomb remains open and treats everyone fairly, he doubles the average sales of other salesmen.[77] I imagine teachers acting as Golomb, delighting in being open to the potential of all students and "making sales" well beyond the average.

Given the hold language has on our perceptions, we need to become aware of how we speak about students. We can begin by developing an awareness of the labels we use. When we hear ourselves saying "low-level" or "high-level," we can choose to stop and rephrase our thinking. When we hear colleagues use these terms, we can reframe the conversation. We can recall classmates, friends, and family who have succeeded beyond expectations and recall those students who surprised us despite our prejudgments. We can remember, too, how we have become smarter through the act of teaching. We know everyone has potential—and when we choose to accept this truth, we will become better teachers.

When we consider the two questions addressed at the beginning of this chapter, "Who's not going to get it?" and "Who will already know it or get it quickly?" we know they apply only to a moment in time—and not to the students themselves.[78]

REFLECTION

When we conveniently label students, we give up on them. The "average" stay average, as they fulfill our expectations earning Cs and Ds, choosing books at their level, and rarely distinguishing themselves. The "bright" keep their place by memorizing for As, rarely taking risks, and often suffering anxiety over grades. Despite efforts to the contrary by dedicated teachers, special education students feel "special," as in "less than" their peers.

Dan Hilliard struggled not to use such terms as "bright," "slow," "honors," and "average." After hearing the two questions posed at the beginning of this chapter, he has begun to reframe his thinking about the potential of his students. In conversations, however, he still occasionally uses such terms, as they were part of the common language in his school. Even parents used them freely, but usually only the positive terms when it came to their own children. He recently read Carol Dweck's *Mindset: The New Psychology of Success*, and was grateful to learn he has a growth mindset both in his life and teaching. He recommended it to his principal for the staff to read.

POINTS TO PURSUE

☑ The tyranny of language! Embedded terms, such as "slow," "bright," "honors," "level one," constrain teachers (and parents) from seeing the potential of each student. Ask yourself—better yet ask colleagues— what keeps us locked into categorizing students? When a student breaks out from our prejudgment, why do we often see it as an anomaly? What can we do to change the conversation?

☑ What difference would it make to teach expecting we will see surprises from our students? To look for the unexpected? Would it help free us from some of our fixed perceptions?

☑ The growth and expansion of special education services assures that struggling students have support throughout their school years. How, then, can we also advocate for those who perform above and beyond our curricula? How will we provide them with challenges to develop their thinking and creativity? Why do we hesitate to acknowledge differences in our classrooms? What can we learn from coaches and teachers in the arts?

☑ How can we learn from the great teachers, such as Jaime Escalante, Marva Collins, and Rafe Esquith, without feeling inferior or threatened by their successes? What can we do on our own to introduce great teaching qualities in ourselves? Can we let go of playing small—"I'm just a teacher"—and step towards greatness? Can we acknowledge the greatness we already have?

☑ As we consider Carol Dweck's two mindsets, can we begin to make a commitment to become more growth minded? If we are to view our students in terms of growth potential, shouldn't we see ourselves in the same way?

☑ The teacher-as-coach analogy offers insights. In *Mr. Holland's Opus*, Glenn Holland denies he's a coach to Lou Russ, an athlete who wants to learn to play a bass drum.[79] Yet, Mr. Holland becomes just that by teaching Lou to play successfully. How does this analogy work for you?

☑ Discuss the following statement, adapted from Marva Collins's student, with colleagues. "I will not judge any student's potential by what he has done in the past or what he's done today. Instead, I will accept what we are not good at as challenges and opportunities for making our brains bigger—mine and my students!" What do you think? How might you rewrite this statement to suit your circumstances?

CHAPTER 12

Abandon the Crabs in the Cage

There is a type of crab that cannot be caught—it is agile and clever enough to get out of any trap. And yet, these crabs are caught by the thousands every day, thanks to particularly human trait they possess.

The trap is a wire cage with a hole at the top. Bait is placed in the cage, and the cage is lowered into the water. One crab comes along, enters the cage, and begins munching on the bait. A second crab joins him. A third. Crab Thanksgiving. Yumm. Eventually, however, the bait is gone.

The crabs could easily climb up the side of the cage and through the hole, but they do not. They stay in the cage. More crabs come in and join them—long after the bait is gone.

Should one of the crabs realize there is no further reason to stay in the trap and attempt to leave, the other crabs will gang up on him and stop him. They will repeatedly pull him off the side of the cage. If he is persistent, the others will tear off his claws to keep him from climbing. If he still persists, they will kill him.

The crabs—by a force of the majority—stay together in the cage. The cage is hauled up, and it's dinnertime on the pier.

Teachers stick together. Given our long history as blue-collar union laborers in factory-model schools, we unite around one another. We develop strong social bonds and loyalties and find strength in our unions. We seldom commit to acting independently even when we think we should. We function, too, in deference to our superiors whether we respect them or not, inside a deeply hierarchical structure. We can hardly imagine administrators as colleagues, let alone see them as necessary supporters of what we do. They are our bosses.

Our deep loyalty to one another, then, serves to protect us from outside threats often perceived as coming from "authorities." In my early years, I listened to colleagues in the faculty room discuss threats to our contracts. We often argued, but when we faced the public we acted as one. I remember, too, how often conversations reverted to complaining.

Take faculty meetings as an example. We learn quickly to dislike them largely because we're forced to attend and because principals run them. So, we rebel and undermine by feigning attention, correcting papers, and carrying on side conversations; once I even fell asleep. We joke about how cleverly we can subvert meetings and roll our eyes to show our disgust. We view these meetings as belonging to administrators, who may begrudge them as much as we do. In some schools, some of us insist on leaving at the precise moment the contract determines, even if the meeting is not finished.

I wonder how much better faculty meetings would be if we took initiative to establish a collegial relationship with the administration. What would happen if we worked with the principal to make the meetings meaningful? Instead of sitting through endless announcements and "administrivia," we could help to design workshops to improve instruction. Imagine the effect of four hours per a month—thirty-six hours per year—of professional learning. Had we had such workshops in my forty years in the classroom, I would have had nearly fifteen hundred hours of collaborative professional learning—and my colleagues and I would have become a more collegial and competent faculty.

We find false solace in complaining about matters such as restrictive schedules, single-letter grading systems, duties, angry parents, uninformed school boards, state mandates, and unmotivated students. Our complaints often become excuses. We lay blame as if we have had no part in creating these problems. We point fingers, but instead we should recognize our complicity in establishing scheduling, grading and reporting systems, and rigid contracts, as we're instrumental in creating the cultures of our schools. It is one matter to complain about what is not working, but it is another to take responsibility for making changes for the better.

We complain, too, about colleagues who do not pull their weight, when we ourselves may be lacking. We allow peers to perpetuate old ways, such as when we stand by at meetings as they put down new teachers' initiatives and voice sharp criticism like, "We do not do this around here," or "We've tried that before and it doesn't work." We feel uncomfortable challenging such comments from colleagues—our friends—so we sit back. We allow the "culture of nice" to prevail, as it assures us a place in the social structure of the school.

Yet, we know this complaining mentality hurts everyone. When our colleagues slight new teachers during faculty meetings, they shut down potential for effective change. They affirm the status quo when they know it needs changing. Soon, new teachers learn to conform, or perhaps as likely, decide to quit.

These situations reflect a crabs-in-a-cage mentality in which everyone sticks close together on the floor of the cage. Any attempt by one to climb out—to make an effort to change—frightens others into pulling him back. By sticking together, we feel safe and build an enclave, one that ironically protects us not only from threats of change but also from the influx of new ideas.

Teacher unions reinforce this mentality. In the early years of factory-designed schools, unions proved important and beneficial, because collective bargaining allowed teachers to advocate for decent wages and working conditions (still a fight for some) and protection from unfair dismissals. But unions have infringed into the business of education, and as a result, have often become a stumbling block for change and innovation. Their role has grown not only in negotiating salaries and benefits, which should be its primary purpose, but also in determining schedules, workloads, job descriptions, and teaching hours.

The union mindset focuses on the security and protection of the group. The practice of harboring less competent members is particularly insidious. I first understood this practice early in my career when an art teacher, who everyone knew was inadequate, garnered public support from the union when the school board held a public hearing to question his competency. Only one staff member was willing to testify in support of dismissal. Nearly as insidious, especially for students, is the reluctance of unions to support innovations unless specified in the teacher contract. Given that most contracts are negotiated for multiple years, they become roadblocks for change. "If it is not in the contract," the argument states, "we cannot and will not consider it until we renegotiate."

In some districts the union hierarchy exerts a stranglehold on its membership. When anyone attempts to act outside the contract, the hierarchy invokes the crabs-in-the-cage principle. We all have heard examples of union officials chastising members for wanting to paint their own classrooms (even when maintenance refuses) or for arranging to hold parent conferences outside specified contract times. We know, too, of districts in which union leadership manages to stay in office for years and enacts frequent grievance procedures to block any and all proposals for changing instructional practice. In some districts, past presidents maintain control years beyond their time in office.[80]

Tenure has become another obstacle that prevents creativity and independence. We spend our first few years on probation, proving our worth (mainly by staying out of trouble), so we can secure a professional contract or tenure. Ironically, assessments during these years often focus on our behavior and not on the quality of instruction. Unlike college and university professors who must prove their academic credentials to earn tenure, teachers need only do a satisfactory job—or appear to.

When we visit our doctors, we are confident they have kept up up-to-date in their practices, as they have to take periodic recertification exams. If we knew they could earn tenure and be able to practice for life without rigorous recertification, we would choose not to continue as their patients. Yet, we allow the teaching profession to equate tenure with job security, requiring nothing more than collecting professional development credits by attending workshops and courses. We rarely conduct—or allow—serious assessments of our teaching.

I remember attending a brain-research workshop, led by a nationally respected presenter, in which two-thirds of the participants left after lunch to shop rather than complete the workshop; since they had already signed in, they received credit hours for the day. Needless to say, I was embarrassed, not only for the presenter but also for the profession. The presenter shared that such behavior is not unusual.

Once we receive tenure, we are virtually guaranteed a lifetime contract. Those who teach the same subject in the same school, for example, can perform at very different levels and yet expect to have contracts renewed annually, as in the case of one science teacher who taught twenty-eight times as much as another teacher down the hall in the same school.[81]

We know who are the most effective teachers in our schools and who are not. Yet, we rarely consider ourselves as one of the weaker teachers. A principal confirmed this point when she told me that after interviewing all of her teachers, she learned that the weaker ones were always somebody else, and never the teacher being interviewed. And parents know which teachers they want for their children, but often have to count on the luck of the draw.

The crabs-in-the-cage mentality, however, ensures we are treated the same. To begin to change this, we can ask:

How can we break out of this persistence to support mediocrity?

Why don't we pay closer attention to evidence that confirms the centrality of our role in student achievement?

How can we become open to data analysis of performance levels?

Why do we support simplistic satisfactory/unsatisfactory performance rating systems that assure, absurdly, that over 95% of us are guaranteed a satisfactory rating?

Michael Jones, in the *Boston Globe*, sums up the absurdity of this system in one sentence: "At 72 of [Boston's] 135 schools, not a single teacher was given an unsatisfactory evaluation. Fifteen of these are on the state's list of chronically underperforming schools."[82] When we remain hunkered down with the crabs-in-the-cage mentality, we not only perpetuate mediocrity and failed practices, but we also deny the opportunity to identify and verify factors that define greatness.

Dr. William Sanders, now a senior research fellow at the University of North Carolina, designed the seminal Tennessee Value Added Assessment System (TVASS) that provides convincing evidence that teacher effectiveness is the leading factor in student achievement. Sanders claims that teachers are ten to twenty times as significant as the effects of other factors, such as socio-economic status, race, urban versus rural, and heterogeneous versus homogeneous grouping.[83] Whether or not we agree with Sanders's research model and conclusions, we know some of us are better teachers than others. It behooves us to know the difference and then strive to teach as the best among us do.

Other researchers, notably William Damon, lament the passivity and apathy of today's students and the discouragement of teachers.[84]

At the same time, he, too, recognizes teaching as "the very heart of schooling. Because a child's learning requires a framework of guiding relationships . . . the teacher is the single most important resource of any school."[85]

By insisting we keep tenure rather than require performance reviews, we implicitly support a play-it-safe mentality. If students fail to learn, we make the argument they do not try hard enough. "If our good students do well," we contend, "we must be doing something right." Such behavior denies our responsibility to design teaching to meet every type of learner. We need to be willing (in fact required) to take initiatives to improve instruction, to seek and receive feedback, and to support one another when trying to change. We would be wise as a faculty to establish the Golden Toilet Award for any colleague who takes a risk to try something new then fails.[86] When we fail, we at least know we tried. If we never try, we never know if our ideas could improve learning.

At the same time, we should not be afraid to honor teachers who succeed. We can no longer pretend all teachers "are fine" and ignore those who design and implement exceptional practices. Teacher of the Year, even Teacher of the Month, misses the point, as this often becomes more political than instructional. Is there only one teacher worth citing? No, it should become common practice to acknowledge all teachers' good work whenever it appears. Everyone wins, particularly when other teachers learn about the good work of their colleagues and make use of it. Teacher of the Week, Teacher of the Day, Teacher of the Moment—it's a no-brainer, really.

And, why not encourage teachers to share Golden Moments, to celebrate the wonderful times that make our teaching worthwhile, such as breakthroughs with parents and students, new collaborations that open doors among colleagues, and moments when students "get it." Such celebrations bring diversity and exploration into the school culture and move us away from feeling pressure to stay under the radar. Nobody wins when everyone stays at the bottom of the cage.

Ultimately, the crabs-in-a-cage syndrome supports a sub-culture to guarantee jobs. Although we teach in isolated classrooms, we make tacit agreements to teach from the front. We know the accepted behaviors we need to follow so no one will bother us. If we give good grades, especially to "honors" students (particularly in high-powered districts) we will please everyone and avoid complaints. Also, when we limit the number of students we send to the office, the administration will likely view us as effective teachers. In cases where teachers face difficult groups (often from the luck of the draw) administrators become annoyed when students are sent to the office and assume the teacher is doing a poor job—and often prejudge without any in-class observation or offer of help.

Sometimes, when I reflect on the crabs-in-a-cage phenomenon, I understand why we teachers stay there, as we face constant public scrutiny and criticism. Everyone, it seems, has opinions about teaching. When the economy tanks, we are often blamed, but when it thrives we remain invisible. When budgets tighten, we suffer. When state test scores drop, we hear criticism. When parents see problems, they talk as if they know how to fix us; after all, they attended school and believe they know everything about education. And if an administrator does not like what we do, he can make life miserable to the point where we want to quit, and we sometimes do. We find it frustrating when others do not appreciate the complexities of what we do every day. Sticking together helps to assure survival.

In the end, however, this mentality fails to serve us—and ultimately our students. If the accepted culture in a school, for example, advocates that teachers lecture and give quizzes, tests, and papers as the primary assessments, those who want to teach differently will feel resistance. Traditional teachers may express displeasure by calling alternative methods "progressive" or risky. Good students may resist because they do not want to change how they do school, as they have mastered learning by memorizing for tests and writing thoughtless formulaic essays. This mediocrity helps explain why colleges have remedial reading and writing centers. And, it confirms why many students become bored and drop out.

Principals who taught as sages-on-the-stage prefer quiet, orderly classrooms with teachers in front. They also prefer to establish good relationships throughout the building and not to rock the boat. By staying out of classrooms, except for the required scheduled observations and evaluations (which everyone knows are dog-and-pony shows) many principals unwittingly support the crabs-in-the-cage-mentality.

Some principals, however, challenge restrictive school cultures and union contracts. They advocate, for example, walkthroughs, learning walks, or mini-observations—somewhat analogous to hospital grand rounds—where principals and teachers make quick visits to classrooms and provide feedback. These approaches offer promise for breaking through the closed culture of isolated classrooms. In schools using walkthroughs, teachers appreciate the feedback once they trust its intentions. And principals appreciate it too, as they learn what actually happens in classrooms.

Ultimately, this crabs-in-the-cage mentality puts a stranglehold on improving teaching. We need to take responsibility, instead, for teaching at our best. We also need to remember that we are the single most important factor for improving instruction. If we decide to stay on the floor of the cage and agree to conform, we will be committing malpractice.

As author Steven Pressfield writes, "The highest treason that a crab can commit is to make a leap for the rim of the bucket."[87] We need to make this leap every day.

REFLECTION

Dan has conflicting concerns about his union. When he first became a teacher, he joined and participated in union activities and became treasurer for a year. But recently, union leadership has expressed concerns about his radical ideas about teaching. Besides, for example, he frequently meets with parents outside school hours. One of the officers questioned him about this practice, as it is in violation of the contract. He does not confront their concerns but worries about possible conflicts. Meanwhile, he continues to push the envelope.

POINTS TO PURSUE

☑ We can begin to comprehend the crabs-in-the-cage mentality by assessing our perceptions of our union. We need to determine how well it serves our teaching, our primary responsibility, and not only how it serves our contract. We should share our thinking with trusted colleagues.

☑ How might you take leadership as a faculty member in your school knowing you might have to confront the union? Perhaps you could institute the Golden Toilet Award or the Golden Moments concept? It might begin to get people thinking off the floor of the cage.

☑ Seek out like-minded colleagues and together approach the principal to find ways to improve professional learning for everyone. If your union takes a "strict-contract," attitude, try to work around it for as long as possible.

☑ While we certainly do not want to unnecessarily threaten job security, how can we take initiative to raise expectations for all teachers in our school and encourage them "to make a leap for the rim of the bucket"—and to be held accountable for performance? Bringing up such questions takes courage, even when have our students first in mind.

CHAPTER 13

Stop the Interruptions

It has to do with power. Every time anyone shamelessly inter-rupted my class, the message was clear: "My time is more valuable than yours. Whatever you're doing cannot possibly be as vital as whatever I'm doing."[88] *(Coleen Armstrong)*

Why do American teachers struggle to find uninterrupted time to teach? What in the school psyche allows office personnel—principals, guidance, and secretaries—to interrupt lessons either over the public address system (PA) or telephone? What allows janitors to run floor-cleaning machines in the hallways or lawn mowers outside windows while we are teaching? We claim that teachers are the most important piece in a child's education, yet others in the school undermine our efforts.

Coleen Armstrong is right. It is a power struggle but an unnec-essary power struggle, an unjustified power struggle. As successful businesses put customers first so too should schools put teachers and students first. As soon as the principal calls over the PA, the lesson disappears! Depending on the length of the announcement and its content, returning to the lesson, if possible, can take several minutes. "Will the following students please come to the office?" has more emotional impact than announcing a change in the lunch menu. A colleague once told me, that she learned that an average of seven min-utes are lost with each announcement.[89] If five occur during the day, thirty-five minutes of teaching is lost. For a week, that means three hours! For thirty-six weeks, forty-eight hours!

As I read Armstrong's the-emperor-is-not-wearing-any-clothes exposure of this travesty, I recalled the opposite practice in Japan where the classroom is considered sacred, learning takes priority, and no interruptions are tolerated.[90] In contrast, in American schools, where handling interruptions is the order of the day, Japanese visitors are stunned, particularly when the PA (Big Brother?) commands the classroom, or when teachers barge in on one another during lessons.

Perhaps some of the onus of living with interruptions rests on our shoulders. How often do we drop in on each other's classrooms in the middle of the period to borrow something or simply to say hello? How often do we interrupt students arbitrarily? Isn't the assembly-line approach to learning built upon scheduled interruptions? We can argue such conditions are reality, the system within which we have to live. But, aren't we part of that design? Couldn't we become advocates for a new design built more on creative flow than segmented timeframes?

Most of us simply tolerate Armstrong's power-struggle interruptions as a fact of life. But if we think more deeply about this issue, we might change our minds. In her article in *Phi Delta Kappan*, Lorraine Hong offers a different perspective, more subtle and perhaps more insidious.[91] Hong describes how increasing intrusions caused her to lose her passion for teaching. As part of an hour-long writing period, fifth-grade teachers were told to include ten minutes of keyboarding. While administrators considered this a simple request, by the time the computers were set up and students settled, it took fifteen to twenty minutes to implement. A new math curriculum was put in place that required teaching sixty minutes per day. Hong found it impossible to schedule it on Mondays and Fridays, because students were required to leave for "gifted" programs and for special education pullouts. She summed up her frustrations with an apt analogy:

> When the days are fragmented and move at the pace of fast-food eateries rather than four-star restaurants, teachers have no time in which to build the provocative experiences that nourish layered learning—experiences that provide teachers with the continuing intellectual and creative challenges that allow them to be professional educators rather than short order cooks.[92]

Four-star restaurants—what a way to visualize classrooms! So contrary to the hamster-wheel-driven lessons, spinning endlessly without comprehension because of pressures from the No Child Left Behind act (NCLB), state assessments, and overcrowded curriculums. Hong and Armstrong together articulate what most of us accept as part of school culture, but in fact contribute stress and anxiety for our students and us. We can, if we choose, decide to combat these interferences, and in Armstrong's words, take back our classrooms.

We can and must take initiative to change this interruptive

culture. We need to be the voice demanding quality education. Instead of accepting every addition to the curriculum, for example, we need to determine whether it belongs and if something else could be dropped. Building patchwork curricula—which adds more material to teach without taking anything away—increases quantity but decreases quality. Teaching mile-wide-inch-deep curricula reduces learning, in contrast to in-depth investigations based on big ideas, active literacy, critical thinking, and thoughtful assessments.

And, every time we interrupt engaged learning to say, "It's time to put away your materials" or "You need to leave now," we send the wrong message. Students quickly learn that working fast and getting the right answers in these short learning segments makes for success. Analytical thinking, reflective conversation, and interactive processing need time to develop if long-term learning is to take root.

Another form of interruption creeping its way into classrooms comes from cell phones and BlackBerries. In classes where students are allowed to have these devices with the notification feature on, students are provoked to respond no matter the task they are working on in the classroom. The research is clear that such interruptions delay returning to the task at hand by as much as fifteen minutes and disrupt coding short-term memory into long-term memory. In addition, filling in "dead time" with electronic communication precludes the daydreaming from which eureka ideas can arise.[93] In a class where students are constantly referring to text-messages, any chance of developing thinking and creative ideas is nearly impossible.

When we allow interruptions to rule, learning retreats to the back burner and conforming to the schedule moves to the front. When the intercom announces the afternoon athletic games during the last ten minutes of a class, the priorities are clear. When a secretary calls over the intercom to ask for student health forms, teaching and learning grind to a halt. When a student turns to the messages on his cell phone, he's no longer in class. Any ideas that were waiting to be discovered disappear.

When I brought this issue before a group of beginning teachers, they understood the problem as obvious—but inevitable. After all, they had lived through its perturbations in their first few months. During our discussion, different viewpoints emerged. Sean, a music teacher, said he felt interruptive when he had to pull out students for lessons and rehearsals. Mary, a special education teacher concurred, and her colleagues nodded in agreement. Several of the classroom teachers listed the innumerable occasions when students left their rooms. Conflicts with "specials" became the central concern for both the classroom teacher and the specials' teachers, but for different reasons. Everyone, however, acknowledged that having to work with fragmented schedules ultimately hurt all parties, especially students.

In the spirit of Coleen Armstrong's power struggle, and a "take back the night" mentality, we need to take back our classrooms. Instead of "acknowledging the inevitable," as my new teachers admitted, we need to define and claim our space, declaring quality instruction as the first priority. As the primary decision-makers for what should be taught, and when and how it should be taught, we must also make class time with students sacred and meaningful. Once the school day begins, we must make instruction the centerpiece of our classrooms.

While issues of curricular interruptions discussed by Hong are more challenging and difficult to overcome, we can begin with what we can directly control: Lawn mowers, vacuums, snow blowers, the public address system, and cell phones (ours included) must remain silent during lessons. And no unannounced visitors are permitted. No exceptions.

How can we resolve this matter? We can begin by joining with colleagues to gather data for a specified amount of time (for example, a month) by recording all interruptions in a given time period. If possible, we should note what happens to our lessons during such times. Once we collect evidence, we should compile the data and bring it to the attention of the administration and ask for help to eliminate or reduce all interruptions. Bringing evidence to support our concerns moves the conversation away from complaining to one voicing concern for improving conditions for instruction.

I cannot imagine the PA operating during class time if everyone declared it off limits; many schools already function without it, including large high schools.[94] I cannot imagine any office staff, guidance counselor, administrator, or fellow teacher entering a classroom uninvited during a lesson if we have declared this behavior unacceptable. One exception is walkthroughs, or learning walks, which are acceptable only if they are integral to the system of instruction in the school and are well understood by teachers and students alike. Finally, maintenance personnel who operate cleaning machines in hallways or mow the lawn outside classroom windows will have to do so before or after school.

A possible side benefit of a no-interruptions policy is that administrative staff could become more involved in classroom teaching, which would reduce class size for everyone. For example, college guidance counselors could schedule classes for application preparation instead of calling individual students out of classes throughout the day. A principal might find time to teach a class in his subject area. Any time the administration participates in the teaching process, it reinforces the message of the classroom as the focus of the school.

Another idea I learned (from where I'm not sure) reduces interruptions for elementary teachers. Instead of scheduling the arts, music, computer, and physical education (PE) "specials" for grades 1–5 every day, a school arranged to have "specials" for each grade all on one day. Not only do teachers have uninterrupted days on the other four, but they also had the opportunity to collaborate one day per week! Perhaps schools could schedule specials to occur only on two days and then plan on two half-days for collaborative planning. We would then achieve two essential changes in the culture of the school: interruptions *and* isolation reduced!

Classrooms ultimately belong to students and should be considered learning sanctuaries. Once we recognize this principle and remember the precious little time we have to create effective learning opportunities, we will not tolerate interference. We already contend with far too many outside dictates that cut into our ability to teach effectively—including excessive interruptions to administer standardized tests. As long as we are complicit with an interruptive school culture, we will perpetuate short-segment teaching resulting in short-term learning. By deciding to reduce interruptions as much as possible, we set in motion the primary imperative of the classroom. It's up to us, then, to use this time wisely.

Perhaps Principal Tim Healey said it best after observing a secretary making an all-school PA announcement on a trivial matter: "Mediocre schools make decisions that are based on what is convenient for secretaries and administrators. Great schools make decisions that maximize and guard instructional time."[95]

REFLECTION

Dan Hilliard discovered early on the deleterious effect of his school's PA system. At least three times per day, the office would make announcements including requesting forms, announcing team bus schedules and after school events, and occasionally broadcasting a message from the principal. He noticed how difficult it was to bring his students back to the lesson, especially when they had been deeply engaged.

When discussing it with more veteran teachers, they told him "it's the way it is." But Dan could not let it go. He conferred with his team and together they agreed to count how many interruptions came from the office (and maintenance) and to use stopwatches to time how long. If possible, they would also try to time how long it took for students to regain focus, a more difficult task.

After several weeks, they collected their data and brought it to the principal. They were pleasantly surprised when he realized the severity of the problem. He promised he would do his part to end interruptions from the office, except at specified times at the beginning and the end of the day. He surprised them when he asked if they and any others would like to study the interruption issue further and include curriculum, specials, and extra-curricular areas. While it meant more work for them, they agreed, as they wanted to make classroom life better for everyone.

"What a difference it would make," Dan said to Angela, "if we could count on teaching without any interruptions. Not only would we be able to teach more effectively, but students would have more opportunity to become more deeply involved as well!"

POINTS TO PURSUE

☑ If your school has interruption issues as described by Coleen Arm-strong, do what Dan and his team did and document the interruptions. Once you collect your data, approach the principal. Have a backup plan if you believe she will resist.

☑ Step back and observe your day through Lorraine Hong's eyes to identify those times when curricular or personnel allocations create interruptions. Can you make some changes to reduce those interruptions? Have discussions with colleagues to see what you can do to make learning smoother—to make your classrooms four-star restaurants.

☑ What can we do to make our classroom a sanctuary for learning? How do we create the self-respect necessary to make this possible? We need to recognize that such classrooms come from being honored from the inside as well as from the outside. How do we teach students to understand that not being allowed to respond to cell phones and BlackBerries during class will improve learning?

☑ Given the randomness of when students leave for "specials," can you help to create a more consistent system, so teachers and students can have longer uninterrupted time periods? Perhaps each grade could have either the morning or the afternoon scheduled two days per week. When we make uninterrupted teaching our priority, we begin thinking about different possibilities and configurations even inside our classrooms.

☑ Visualize yourself as a teacher in a four-star classroom. What is already there? What else do you need? What interferes, making you feel more like a short order cook? What do you need to discard? How might electronic devices "feed" a four-star classroom?

CHAPTER 14

End One-Size-Fits-All Teaching

"I think I used to be more like Mr. Appleton, because I gave a lot of lectures. But now, I am more like Mrs. Baker, as I do many fun activities as well as some lecturing. I'm afraid I do not use many of the ideas of Ms. Cassell."

"I agree, I'd like to be more like Ms. Cassell, but I think I would have to be careful if I wanted to have a life outside of the classroom!"

Teachers like to talk about themselves. In my ten years teaching teachers, I have asked participants in my Differentiated Instruction course to write a reflection about themselves as teachers after reading Carol Ann Tomlinson's now-classic essay, "Mapping a Route Towards Instruction."[96]

Tomlinson develops her essay around three teachers who all teach about ancient Rome.

Mr. Appleton represents the classic stand-up, one-size-fits-all teacher who uses a textbook, has students read the text in class and take notes, and lectures frequently, expecting students to take notes then, as well. He gives out study sheets before tests.

Mrs. Baker introduces graphic organizers to help students read the textbook. She brings in pictures, invites students to wear togas, and to bring food for a Roman banquet. Also, she shows video clips on gladiators and reads myths to her students. She goes over the chapter before the test rather than making them do it at home.

Ms. Cassell plans her year using long-range thinking, concentrating on a few key concepts and generalizations, sets clearly defined facts and skills, provides multiple pathways to learn material, and develops essential questions to drive the thinking. Her classroom is more unified, more intricate, and more complex than the other two teachers' classrooms.

The teachers in my courses say they see themselves in various combinations of all three teachers. Many state that they used to teach like Mr. Appleton but have moved over to Mrs. Baker's approach in an attempt to make their classrooms more appealing to more students. Few say they emulate Ms. Cassell—many see the value of her approach but, at the same time, say she should "get a life" because of how much she attempts and accomplishes!

Usually our conversations center around the issue of coverage. Participants point out the need to cover as much as possible to prepare for state assessments, so to teach like Ms. Cassell would take too much time. "It would be nice to be able to become Ms. Cassell," some say, "just like it was before the state tests, when we could spend time teaching what we enjoyed."

The irony, I point out, is that this reasoning ignores not only the increasing alienation of students from teaching as talking, but it also ignores the conclusions of research. The National Research Council's definitive compilation on brain research states, "teachers must teach some subject matter in depth, providing many examples in which the same concept is at work and providing a firm foundation of factual knowledge."[97] Teachers instinctively understand this idea but, as we've seen, feel trapped under pressure from state assessments.

The problem remains that "coverage" does not guarantee learning or retention. When we choose to explain, we become the major beneficiaries of our explanations. No matter how well we explain, there's no guarantee students will learn; but if we allow them to explain what they know to us, we will know they have learned. But we feel caught: "If I don't cover what *might* be on the test, my students will not have an opportunity to learn it. When I cover everything in a mile-wide-inch-deep approach, I recognize not many will retain it. At least I can defend that I have done my job and covered what needed to be covered." But, as a colleague shared with me, when we teach something and students do not learn, then nothing happened![98]

By the time we end our conversation about Mr. Appleton, Mrs. Baker, and Ms. Cassell, we usually reach an impasse. Still, the elephant in the room has been exposed, as the central question underlying this book emerges: "What can I do every day to make significant learning happen for each and every student in my classroom?" Our students will have little chance to become learners if we fail to create coherent curricula, units of study, and lessons.

If we choose to perpetuate Mr. Appleton's stand-up pedagogy, our digitally-wired students will be destined for boredom and disinterest, except for those few who can learn from lectures and note taking. If we choose to emulate Mrs. Baker's activity-centered teaching, our lessons will be interesting, but without coherence or direction. Students may enjoy the learning, but will not be able connect the dots, as we bounce from one activity to the next. However, if we choose Ms. Cassell's approach, we are in for more work, but we are also in for more satisfaction, as each lesson, each unit, and the whole year will be sequenced and will include carefully chosen knowledge and skills, principles of learning, and essential questions to drive thinking.[99]

Agreeing that Ms. Cassell's approach is the way to proceed does not guarantee we will move away from the pedagogies of Mr. Appleton and Mrs. Baker. As I've emphasized throughout this book, these practices are deeply embedded. Making a commitment "to become Ms. Cassell" requires a major overhaul, demanding major changes in our practice—more for some of us and less for others. We can argue that we have no incentive to put in this extra effort, since we will not be recognized nor receive more pay. Ironically, perhaps some of us will succumb to pressure from colleagues not to change but keep doing as we have always done—the crabs-in-the-cage syndrome.[100]

Still, the question remains, "What can I do every day to make meaningful learning happen for each and every student in my classroom?" Ultimately, it becomes a question of diversifying our teaching, a process beginning by taking small steps in our philosophy and strategies. As a way to introduce the need to diversify, I employ an arm-folding exercise from an idea I learned from a colleague, Jerry Goldberg. I invite participants to:

1. "Fold your arms, please, in your natural way."
2. "Those whose left arm is on top of their right arm, raise your hand." Then, I pause. "You are visual learners."
3. "Those who have the right arm on top, please raise your hand. You are auditory learners."

4. "Anyone who disagrees with this 'research' (which I admit is bogus), raise your hand. You are kinesthetic learners."
5. Then, I ask everyone to fold their arms the opposite way.

After some struggle, most are able to do it but complain it's uncomfortable. I then bring home the obvious point: We all have students whose arms are folded opposite to ours; that is, their ways of learning differ from ours. As teachers, we are obligated to reach out to these differences. We need to respond in ways that enhance each student's learning. We have no choice.

When participants turn to each other and say they want to try this exercise with their students, I know I have made my point.

Once we glimpse the necessity to shift our thinking away from delivery and towards making learning happen for each student, we look for alternative pedagogies, such as the ones in Part I, "What Can We Do Immediately?" If as lecture-teachers we adopt 10-2 Thinking, the structure of our lessons radically shifts from monologue to dialogue.[101] Instead of acting as Mr. Appleton, choose to emulate Dan Hilliard's move into the middle of the room. We open our eyes and ears to the learning happening around us. We leave class having learned alongside our students and return the next day having developed new insights from the interactivity. We choose "purposeful engagement"[102] to enable intelligence to grow for our students and ourselves.

Once we've let go of the Mr. Appleton within us, we need to move quickly beyond Mrs. Baker to Ms. Cassell. For that, we must adopt a backwards-design mindset—planning and teaching with the end in mind—that includes the following elements:

- Our courses, units of study, and lessons need purposeful intention—a clear sense of direction for all involved.

- Our activities should be taught because they belong in an aligned learning sequence, not simply because they are interesting or fun.

- Our teaching builds on previous understandings towards new understandings.

- Our questions should ignite curiosity, intrigue, and significant thinking.
- Our lessons should have objectives clear to everyone.
- Our homework assignments should connect to what's been learned in class.

Each day, then, is all about the fascination of learning, for students and teachers, within a coherent framework.

If we decide instead to keep the textbook at the center of our teaching, we will struggle to make these changes. When we choose to "cover" the text, we become passive, and turning the pages of the text determines the course of our teaching. But, when we step outside the textbook, we begin to prepare better as we take full responsibility for determining what students will know, understand, and be able to do. We become alive in the process. We seek an aligned curriculum so students will learn better. We realize the need to work closely with colleagues to make this possible.

Those of us who rely on workbooks and worksheets also need to reassess their place on the learning continuum, especially at the elementary and middle levels. We remember the myriad of worksheets we, as students, did simply as busywork. For some of us, we did more work because we finished earlier and the teacher needed time to teach the others. For others, the worksheets were simple and kept us occupied. Especially when done alone as seatwork, worksheets rarely taught us anything worthwhile. If I could declare an edict to all teachers, I would say: "Abandon all worksheets—for seatwork and for homework!"

What happens when we decide to make our teaching provocative? What happens to our students? The answers are:

- They stay awake and alert.
- They ponder thoughtful questions and seek answers to build understanding.
- They become curious, and open to the wonder and awe of learning and life.
- They find passion.
- They know they're learning.

Take, for example, two history students. One student sits in a classroom at his desk and writes lecture notes for two weeks, takes a couple of quizzes, and finishes with a test (usually on a Friday) the day after the teacher reviews the material (much like Mr. Appleton). He did the same the previous two weeks and the two weeks before that.

The second student engages in his teacher's directed discussions analyzing and assessing the material focusing, for example, on the complexities of cause and effect and the resulting moral issues of wars. Sometimes the whole class engages; other times everyone works in small groups, in pairs, or in threes. The teacher uses Give One/Get One for review.[103] She sees herself as a coach who assesses her team (class) during the review, then determines how to arrange the equipment (material) for the upcoming game (test).[104]

The first student receives information from the teacher and must take responsibility for learning it outside of class. The second student engages in learning with the teacher, then reviews and reinforces it outside of class. While both students may earn As, the second student will respond better to outside testing—and will retain much more of what he learns. In addition, he will be developing lifelong learning skills.

How can those of us overwhelmed by Ms. Cassell's methods let go of our anxieties and begin to rethink our approach to teaching? We already feel overwhelmed, and if we do everything Ms. Cassell does, we, too, might feel the need to get a life! We can begin to rethink how we teach with the following ideas:

- Instead of planting material into the heads of our students, we devise lessons to engage them in purposeful learning.

- Instead of delivering lectures and collecting frequent quizzes and tests to correct, we include students in creating learning and making assessments.

- Instead of struggling to keep their attention, we engage students in meaningful work.

- Instead of working alone, we plan with our colleagues, observe one another, and share and assess student work together.

Unfortunately, we may have to begin alone. Unlike professional athletes, actors, singers, and others who have personal trainers, we work in one of the few professions without personal coaches, except for those of us lucky to have had mentors in our first year or two. We need to find ways to support one another and provide feedback.

- We can invite colleagues to observe us during their planning periods to give us specific feedback about the quality of our teaching, and offer to do the same for them.

- We can invite administrators to drop by our classrooms informally and provide feedback about where we need help.

- We can ask parents if they are willing to visit and share their observations.

- We can ask students to fill out index cards at the end of each week to let us know what they have learned and what questions they may have.[105]

Ultimately, we must decide whether we will teach as Mr. Appleton, Mrs. Baker, or Ms. Cassell. As teachers, we have a long history of doing what we want in our isolated classrooms. We can carry on as our predecessors and teach one-size-fits-all lessons, or we can accept this invitation to diversify our teaching to meet the learning needs of each student. We can choose the TAPS Template for Teacher Planning[106] as a guide for entering into this commitment. We can, in Tomlinson's words, create our own map towards instruction and seek all the help we can muster to make it happen. We are, after all, the deciders of our classrooms.

REFLECTION

The one-size-fits-all lesson has been the teachers' staple for generations. Dan Hilliard's foray into the middle of the room could be seen as a whole-class lesson, but not in the classic sense. Dan, like most of his colleagues, sat through whole-class lessons in school and college, and—again like most of his colleagues—learned to teach from the front of the room.

The challenge remains to make teaching from the middle of the room become a reality. Dan understands that one-size-fits-all thinking has become oxymoronic in today's global world. He is committed to revamping his teaching to meet his students' needs—and to make his teaching more satisfying.

POINTS TO PURSUE

☑   Where are you on the spectrum of Mr. Appleton, Mrs. Baker, and Ms. Cassell? How did you get there? Are you happy with where you are?

☑   To what extent do you practice one-size-fits-all teaching that focuses on coverage? Have you thought of ways to break away without compromising your perceived obligations to cover what is required? What small steps could you take? Try using the TAPS Template for Teacher Planning. Discuss your ideas with a colleague.

☑   If you have moved closer to Ms. Cassell, how will you convince colleagues not only to let go of one-size-fits-all practices but also to recognize that they will need to work harder? Will they think the benefits to students will be enough incentive?

☑   How would an observer describe students in your class? As passive or active? Some of the time, most of the time, or all of the time? Invite a colleague to observe your class.

PART IV

What Can We Learn from Beyond the Culture of Schools?

If we are to discover our full potential and the potential of our students, we must look beyond the culture of the school and the classroom. We are living in a world that is integrating previously disparate elements at mind-bending speed. If we choose instead to hunker down inside the confines of school thinking, we will soon become anachronistic and irrelevant.

We need to open our minds to ideas from beyond the norm, from beyond the enclave of school culture. We can begin by imagining new and different roles for teachers. We can also reframe our perceptions and accomplish more than we thought possible.

In addition, we can examine our potential to affect the quality of life in the classrooms of newer colleagues. We can deepen our understanding of the ultimate purpose of teaching as it relates to the greater universe within which we live. And, we can take time to imagine the ideal classroom in which we would like to teach.

Expanding our thinking beyond the classroom, beyond the schoolhouse, makes for a better understanding of our place and purpose, and enables us to connect more imaginatively and deeply with our students, and with each other.

CHAPTER 15

Become a Gadfly

We teach alone. From the first day we step into our classrooms, we work without feedback except when supervisors observe or evaluate. Teaching is a private affair subsidized by government—it has been for generations. Rarely do we discuss teaching practices with colleagues. And rarely, if ever, do we observe a colleague or invite them to observe us. It's simply not part of our culture.

Perhaps the images of the dialogical encounters of Socrates on the Acropolis, or of Mark Hopkins, then President of Williams College, sitting on one end of a log and a student on the other, have perpetuated the myth of teaching as an intimate affair. One-room schoolhouses had but one teacher. Factory-model schools constructed buildings with long corridors, with one teacher in each room who was expected to deliver a unified curriculum. No wonder we remain isolated. By spending the school day alone, we are denied opportunities to receive feedback.

Why not, then, introduce the idea of a gadfly on the staff—a teacher without her own classroom who serves all the classrooms in the school? (Hear me out, and suspend your disbelief.) I have often dreamed of taking on this role; this is how I see it:

> I arrive in the morning to my small office, then check my computer
> to see if any teachers have made a request for help. Aha, Mrs. Wilson
> needs the material I promised this morning; the third grade wants help
> planning a trip to our local science museum. I first go to Mrs. Wilson's
> fourth grade with the requested material, ready to teach a lesson. She
> decides to stay, and talks with me after about her impressions and ideas
> for continuing with her students. I then proceed to the third grade to
> meet with the team to plan the museum trip . . .
>
> Throughout the day I rove as an observer, questioner, commentator,
> teacher, co-teacher, seminar leader, and idea person; I float by invitation
> from room to room. I help to make learning possible by advocating
> for meaningful, exciting, rigorous, engaging, humorous, stimulating,
> and worthwhile learning—for students and teachers. I imagine helping
> teachers to purge outmoded methods, to implement best practices, and

to create new ones. I create feedback loops. I am not a judge. Instead, I become a pied piper among my peers.

As a gadfly, I break down the generational isolation that limits us, and find ways to release our gifts to one another. I see colleagues interacting on many levels by talking about teaching, creating new ideas, and designing aligned curriculums. When I take over a class at a teacher's request, she either chooses to stay, or decides to spend time with a colleague, or prepares on her own. I create opportunities for ad hoc conversations to develop collegiality.

As my homework, I reflect on the day and look for web resources, materials, books, articles, and people in response to staff needs and requests. Before going to bed, I either email or text, if necessary, and prepare what to bring the next day.

I break down the isolation—unwittingly self-imposed—surrounding all of us . . .

The overarching purpose of a gadfly as described here, is to support and nurture creative possibilities for learning. In essence, the gadfly provides the feedback that gives colleagues the tools and confidence to teach so that all students learn. She also takes part in leading staff meetings to assure that matters concerning teaching remain central in the conversations.

To sustain this idea, however, the gadfly should come from within a faculty, perhaps as a rotating one-to-three-year appointment, or as an in-school sabbatical. With a gadfly, the school's culture will change. The isolation will break down. Teacher initiative will become more commonplace. Active professional relationships will develop and evolve into professional learning communities or self-management teams—teachers working together on common concerns. Collaboration allows the whole to be greater than the sum of its parts.

Having a gadfly on staff breaks down the endemic isolation of teachers. She assures that they collaborate to:

- Activate lessons to excite and engage students
- Discuss different options for struggling students
- Provide alternative materials to our advanced students in a particular topic

- Group students flexibly during lessons to improve learning
- Teach students to self-assess
- Respond to different learning styles, particularly those different from our own
- Apply brain research to improve student learning
- Arrange and rearrange desks to facilitate lessons
- Summarize to build long-term retention
- Provide challenging and worthwhile alternative products for students to demonstrate what they have learned
- Frame lessons so students will be more aware of what they are learning and why
- Create essential questions to stimulate thinking and motivate learning

Imagine the effect of receiving feedback from one of our own, a teacher as gadfly, whose desire is to make all of us better! Imagine the effect on the gadfly herself, who finally has an opportunity to share her pent-up ideas! We all need help. We cannot teach alone any more. Great teaching demands that every time we step into our classrooms we address the central question I pose in this book, "What can I do every day to make meaningful learning happen for each and every student in my classroom?" Invoking this question invites us to seek answers. We set our intention—and the gadfly is there to make it possible.

Alone, we struggle to let go of treating students as targets needing improvement, as regurgitating robots who can pass tests. But together, we can make lifelong learning central to our teaching. An ever-present gadfly, as a catalyst, would help us break the teach-to-the-test paradigm and connect us to new and best practices.

The gadfly as a member of staff without a classroom becomes a member of everyone's classroom, an insider who helps to improve teaching. The gadfly's presence validates not only our *need* to improve practice, but also our *ability* to succeed. The gadfly, ultimately, affirms we not only have the skills to teach to make learning happen but also the will to do it.

REFLECTION

The design of schools, as we've seen, places administrators at the top of a hierarchy with teachers below, and below them are paraprofessionals. The term "superintendent" reflects the factory-based origins of the public school. Dan Hilliard naturally expected his principal to be in charge of his teaching. Surprisingly, his principal never appeared in his classroom during his first five years of teaching. He told Dan he hired him because he came from a well-respected college and already had his master's degree. Fortunately, his department chair visited him often and offered to co-teach one of his classes. Now, his principal is required to evaluate new teachers twice a year for the first three years.

Still, Dan was frustrated. He knew he needed feedback if he was to improve. When he heard the idea of teacher-as-gadfly, he became excited. After all, he was somewhat of an idealist! Yet, how would such a position be funded, he wondered? How could the district be made to fund it, when budgets are tight? Still, the idea of a gadfly opened him to try to find ways to create feedback loops among his peers.

POINTS TO PURSUE

☑ Suspend your own disbelief and explore the potential of appointing a gadfly to work your school. How might this be arranged? Who might be willing and capable of doing it? Should the school hire an outsider to begin this practice? How would you advocate for this position in the budget?

☑ What if, instead, you and some like-minded colleagues agreed to become gadflies for one another? For example, if you were a department head, how might you restructure your position to act as a gadfly? Who could take up the administrative tasks of your job? Perhaps you could do it for selected time periods, for example, for a week each month. Perhaps, you could "gadfly" during your planning periods?

☑ Perhaps simply bringing up the possibility of a gadfly on staff might inspire teachers to become more willing to open their doors to one another. At least, that might be a start.

CHAPTER 16

Leverage Tipping Points

Malcolm Gladwell puts readers in touch with key ideas in our culture. In *The Tipping Point*, he asserts that social change can happen quickly with little input, in the same way viruses cause epidemics—what he calls tipping points. This concept explains radical change under the right circumstances. He compares it to a measles epidemic in kindergarten when one child introduces the virus, which immediately spreads to everyone, reaches a critical mass, then quickly runs its course. A situation may be placid one moment and explosive the next.[107]

Having become a teacher eager to break its sterile patterns, I have yet to see much change. As I have articulated, we teachers continue to teach much as we always have. Even when we work alongside a colleague who creates new ways to reach students, we rarely adopt her ideas. We reside in a deeply conservative profession, determined, so it seems, to be who we were. As a teacher of teachers, I am still baffled about how to crack this barrier, but I intend for this book to provide a wedge.

I have seen teachers create innovations that never make their way into neighboring classrooms. A teacher in a team develops an effective contract to guide classroom behavior, but her colleagues do not adopt it and continue to have behavior issues. Another finds ways to escape the tyranny of the textbook, only to be shunned by colleagues. Constructivism, which has roots in Dewey, Piaget, and Vygotsky, remains largely unknown among teachers. The Progressive and Open Education movements faltered before they could find a foothold in schools. Montessori's rich successes remain largely outside the reach of public classrooms. Two relatively recent approaches, "differentiated instruction" to improve teaching methods and "backwards design" to improve planning, are slowly making inroads but remain largely unknown and unpracticed; perhaps they will reach a tipping point—we'll have to see.

I ponder the following questions as I present professional learning workshops and courses to teachers:

- Why do efforts of innovative colleagues fail to take hold—and more likely are actively resisted?

- Why haven't new ideas—even good old ideas—spread as viruses?

- What prevents us from responding to off-the-wall ideas, trying them out, and adopting what works?

- What keeps most of us where we are, year after year, generation after generation? (Gladwell claims peer pressure acts as a powerful inhibitor. I have taken off-beat paths at different times in my career only to find myself isolated either by standing alone among colleagues or by being rebuked by those in charge. I felt like the crab in the cage trying to escape, but no one would let me.)[108]

- Is it possible to create tipping points as individual teachers?

- What good comes from introducing new strategies to faculties if teachers do not change?

- What points would tip teachers—and schools—into becoming more successful with all their students?

- How do we make worthwhile ideas contagious?

Most of the teachers in my workshops appear thoughtful about teaching—and certainly know what they could do differently if they made the choice. (Some, as presenters well know, resist *any* ideas we introduce.) But as consultants, we rarely know if any of the ideas will tip them towards a different direction, towards more engagement, towards more learning in the classroom. Perhaps we do spark change. Perhaps we set tipping points in motion in classrooms, hopefully as "viruses" to cause learning. Perhaps.

I decided to become a teacher of teachers after a long career, primarily because I wanted to press for teacher reform as I've done from my first days in the classroom. I joke with a friend of mine, Barbara Barnes, now in her mid-eighties, about how both of us entered schools desiring to change teaching, and despite our apparent lack of success, we haven't given up! I imagine myself in my eighties still at it, as she is.

Occasionally, I have opportunities to give keynote speeches to whole faculties. Despite the obvious challenges of effecting change as an outside speaker, I take it seriously. I begin by imagining sitting in the audience and listening to what I say. I see my talk as a chance to infuse ideas to inspire teachers to make their classrooms lively, happening places.

Sometimes, I share the four principles of Pike's Place Fish Market in Seattle. (The market has inspired workplaces throughout the country with their fresh and zany actions; for instance, they throw fish—big ones!—to customers.) Their four principles are:

Choose your attitude
Play
Be present
Make someone's day[109]

These principles reflect my convictions as a teacher:

- I enter class knowing I can be upbeat about my students and circumstances regardless of how I felt yesterday.

- I can put playfulness—in my case puns—into my lessons, instead of always being serious about the business of learning.

- I can be fully present with my students' responses, instead of being present only with my teachings.

- I can certainly bring a smile to a student in way that, in turn, uplifts everyone.

Taken seriously, these principles can radically shift attitudes, particularly in larger and more impersonal schools. Sometimes, I am naïve enough to believe that the act of describing Pike's Place in my presentation will flip a happiness switch as if it were a transforming tipping point. But, I realize how fleeting my efforts are as soon as the principal takes the microphone to list things to do before sending teachers off to their rooms. (When I returned to one school, however, a teacher gave me a Pike's Place Fish Market hat as he grinned from ear to ear. The message stuck, at least for him!)

In other keynotes, I sometimes focus on the power of redirecting intention; that is, by making the assumption that when we intend to teach differently, we will. I invoke the words of Paul Hawken, "We have no control of the outcome . . . the only thing we can control is our intent."[110] Setting our intention offers a way, perhaps, of implanting tipping points, one change at a time, to spur further changes until only remnants of poor past practices remain. The intention itself is not a tipping point, but enacting the intention may set it in motion.

But as we've seen in the rider and elephant metaphor,[111] making radical changes takes time, patience, and support. When we make new intentions but are forced to work alone, we have few, if any, opportunities to find support and feedback. We face students who are used to school as we experienced school; parents who expect school to be as it was for them; and administrators in many schools who prefer orderly, well-run buildings, which usually means business as usual. Creating tipping points in this atmosphere may be almost impossible.

Still, I believe Gladwell's idea has relevance. During one of my keynotes, I began to believe I was tipping teachers towards possibilities rather than the same old same old. I shared the Pike's Place principles and Paul Hawken's intention, plus a few ideas of my own, in the late morning; I lunched with several teachers; then I led a follow-up session in the early afternoon. Several people came to me afterward to share their excitement, including how they intended to use some of the ideas. The administrator who hired me, however, departed within a month after school began, and another left before Thanksgiving. Not much possibility of enduring tipping points there.

Chip and Dan Heath's *Made to Stick: Why Some Ideas Survive and Others Die*,[112] grew out of Gladwell's stickiness concept. As the book's title indicates, the authors focus on sticky ideas, ones that are easily understood, remembered, and affect change. They developed five principles using the acronym, SUCCESs:

- Simplicity: determine and prioritize your core message and communicate it using an analogy or high-concept pitch; keep it simple, don't dumb down.

- Unexpected: gain and hold attention creating curiosity gaps to make students want your message; use exciting lead-ins, dynamic questions, and mystery queries.

- Concrete: use sensory language (for example, Aesop's fables), paint a mental picture, employ the Velcro theory of memory as having multiple hooks; specificity connects.

- Credible: ideas gain legitimacy from outside authorities (or anti-authorities) or from within using human-scale statistics (for example, one child for Save the Children or the Smile Train); let students test it out before they buy.

- Emotional: people care about people, not numbers; be aware as identity appeals can often trump self-interest.

- Stories: drive action through simulation (what to do), inspiration (the motivation to do it), and springboard stories (helping others see how an existing problem might change).[113]

The Heaths are onto something—and they have written with teachers in mind. Any teacher who takes their message to heart, reads the book, and makes use of their website cannot enter a class again and fail to wonder how to make his teaching stick. Already, students enter our classrooms full of sticky ideas, most of which have no use for them or for us. But, if we decide to appeal to the stickiness in their brains, we will break the cycles of monotony—and no longer require them sit passively.

Already, teachers tell me they are looking for more sticky ways to conduct courses and lessons. Perhaps each of us has tipping points ready to be awakened or released. Surely, when we let go of acting as conduits of an imposed curriculum, we will take ownership of what we teach. We will transform the minds and hearts of our students. We will invoke an epidemic of learning in our classrooms.

If we are reluctant to consider ourselves as potential tipping point providers, we might heed the words of Martha Graham:

There is a vitality, a life force, an energy, a quickening that is translated through you into action, and because there is only one of you in all time, this expression is unique. And if you block it, it will never exist through any other medium and it will be lost. The world will not have it. It is not your business to determine how good it is nor how valuable nor how it compares with other expressions. It is your business to keep it yours clearly and directly, to keep the channel open.[114]

Imagine a school full of teachers who have a "vitality, a life force, a quickening," who view themselves as tipping-point contributors. How would they interrelate? What would be happening in their classrooms? How would students feel? What would they be learning? Perhaps the intention to become a tipping-point provider is actually enough to become a tipping point!

REFLECTION

Dan read Gladwell's *Tipping Point*, but had not figured out how to connect it to his lessons. When he discovered *Made to Stick*, however, his mind jumped. He already used stories, which always perked his students' curiosity. He had tried concrete and specific approaches, but realized he often slipped into the abstract, which appealed only to some students. The key revelations of *Made to Stick* forced him to choose his priorities and keep it simple. He recommended the book to the principal for the faculty to read, but hasn't heard back.

POINTS TO PURSUE

☑ Think of a teacher you know who operates out of the box. Perhaps you are one. What happens in your school to this teacher (or to you)? Consider how you can be a catalyst to spread out-of-the-box ideas into neighboring classrooms, down the hall, and in the building.

☑ Commit to trying an out-of-the-box idea each week. Process how it worked (or not) with your students. Inviting them in on your efforts to make learning more interesting will encourage them to ratchet up their efforts.

☑ Explore the implications of implementing the four principles of Pike's Place Fish Market in your classroom. Plan carefully how you'd launch them (check the Web, or buy one of their books, *Fish!* or *When Fish*

Fly), and carefully observe the effects. How might you introduce these principles to colleagues?

☑ Setting new intentions can be difficult. As stated, you will need patience and support. As Paul Hawken said, "We have no control of the outcome . . . the only thing we can control is our intent." If you choose this path, be willing to persist!

☑ Make a plan to study *Made to Stick* (the book and the Website, http://www.madetostick.com), preferably with colleagues. Dig in and try out its six ideas. Be open with students about what you are doing. My bet is they will respond, particularly if you've been doing most of the talking.

☑ Have you ever thought of a new way to teach but dismissed it as too far out of the box? Resurrect that idea and try it again. Perhaps it will have an impact and become a tipping point, perhaps not. If not, give yourself the Golden Toilet award for taking a risk and failing.[115]

CHAPTER 17

Teach As If

When we live in our teaching, ideas arrive as if from nowhere. Once, I heard the story of a man who never could remember how to swipe his card on the bus on the way to work. Each day, the driver or other passengers helped him. It turned out he later won a Nobel Prize. Do we have future Nobel Prize winners before us in our classrooms, among students who do not seem to have a clue much of the time? Who are we teaching?

Ideas feed my teaching and many of the most memorable have come from beyond the classroom. David Attenborough's *Gandhi* reoriented my perspective and purpose as a teacher. My mother's gift of Benjamin Hoff's *The Tao of Pooh* became a classic for teaching Taoism to my eighth graders. Ideas surround us and wait for our perusal. Recently, one came from an interview in *The New Yorker* with Philip Pullman, who argued for pursuing what matters in the face of those who wish to control all we do. He calls them "theocracies . . . the tendency of human beings to gather power to themselves in the name of something that may not be questioned."[116]

Theocracies. Unquestioned leadership. I have not thought much about this since teaching history years ago. And here was Philip Pullman taking them on. I realize I have engaged in this conversation with authorities from my first days of teaching. Sometimes, I even imagined I'd won. Pullman admits in his argument that theocracies eventually win out, but

> That doesn't mean we should give up and surrender . . . I think we should act *as if.* I think we should read books, and tell children's stories, and take them to the theatre, and learn poems, and play music, as if it would make a difference . . . We should act as if the universe were listening to us and responding. We should act as if we were going to win . . . [117]

Perhaps that's how I thought of myself in the classroom. I acted "as if" I would not succumb, "as if" I could be me despite an authority relegating me to a lesser position. Perhaps my spirit insisted that I be who I am no matter the circumstances. When the superintendent dissolved my middle school progressive classroom into a traditional format, I returned to teaching social studies in a departmentalized team without skipping a beat. I did not win, but acted "as if" I had.

We survive as teachers, in part, because we've long appeased the theocracies, which originated in the factory-designed schools of the early twentieth century. We often resisted reform efforts by acting "as if" we've reformed. Yet, we still reside at the bottom of a hierarchical ladder, and despite working alone in private, isolated classrooms, we defer to those at the top. We perpetuate an "us versus them" relationship. What if instead we believe that we are the key deciders in our classrooms? (We are, of course!) What if we act "as if" we are in charge and become decision-makers, not only in our classrooms but also our schools? Why not act "as if" we have an active role in governing our schools, as our university colleagues do? What might happen?

Taking Pullman's counsel, we can create a sense of empowerment for us and for our students. We could model, as well, the role of active learners by asking provocative questions and pondering outcomes. Teaching "as if" would encourage us to teach to make worthwhile learning happen for every child, irrespective of the often bogus requirements and demands of oppressive theocracies.

As I look back on my teaching years, I wonder why only some of us risked invoking "as if" possibilities. Why did we choose to take part in offbeat methodologies rather than fulfill implied mandates? Why did we feel called to do it our own way rather than do what we were "expected" to do? Sometimes we gained company, but even when we felt alone, we liked being different. Choosing the "as if" path created meaning.

Shortly after reading the Pullman piece, I discovered Eliot Eisner's "deep stuff that schools should teach"—five ideas to push the boundaries of orthodoxy of schools:

- Judgment—students deal in problems having more than one answer
- Critical thinking—exploring big ideas "with legs"
- Meaningful literacy—reading, writing, numeracy—"*and*" music, visual arts and dancing

- Collaboration—moving beyond solo performance to mean-ingful collaborative work during school

- Service—students learning to reach out beyond individual achievement to the community at large[118]

Eisner invites us to step out from under theocratic thinking. What if we took his five ideas to heart? What would we do differently? Certainly his framework asks us to invite students to explore rather than to regurgitate, to investigate rather than to repeat, and to learn in community rather than to compete for grades.

If we taught "as if" Eisner's five principles mattered, imagine our excitement in teaching to solve complex problems instead of giving notes to copy. Imagine inviting students to write reflections in class in response to unresolved issues, instead of only writing at home. Imagine connecting with the greater world rather than pursuing textbook chapters that lack any narrative. Imagine teaching for learning rather than for test taking.

Yet, we hesitate to implement frameworks like Eisner's, because it would take time away from covering material. As previously noted, we feel pressured to teach fast. But, these five ideas offer yet another invitation to let go of coverage, and trust uncoverage and exploration to better serve our students. Taking such a position, however, puts us outside of the prevalent theocracy. Given the pressures of NCLB and state assessments, making such a decision is difficult.

Eisner is one of a growing number of educators calling for teachers to concentrate on learning. Robert Marzano, whose exemplary research calls for significant reform, articulates ten questions to direct us away from the tyranny of the coverage theocracy in his book, *The Art and Science of Teaching.* The questions address critical areas for us to consider as we teach from the middle of the room, including communicating goals, accessing new knowledge, engaging students, establishing rules and positive relationships, and holding high expectations.[119]

Imagine using one of Marzano's questions to guide discussions about teaching with colleagues. Imagine how these questions would help us tap into our understandings of the teaching process and our purpose. Imagine how we would change as a result of these conversations. Imagine what would happen to theocracies.

Perhaps when we act "as if," we need to heed again Pullman's words and ". . . act as if the universe were listening to us and responding. We should act as if we were going to win . . ." After all, the universe is listening. When we teach "as if," it is listening and responding, our students listen as we listen, and they respond as we respond. Together, we act "as if" we are going to win. We can be free to teach our hearts out. We can find confidence in our purpose, in our invitations to learn, in our celebrations, in our integrity, and in living our truths to make a difference in ways we may otherwise never realize.

If we decide to implement these ideas, we will need to believe in ourselves as teacher decision-makers—at least act "as if" we believe— and feel assured that our students will be the beneficiaries as they become lifelong learners—this is essential for their future.

So much happens when we live in our teaching. What appears outside our domain suddenly can have relevance as we see connections, insights, and serendipity. When powerful ideas appear, such as Philip Pullman's "as if" and Eliot Eisner's five principles, they open the door to new possibilities. They also remind us not to assume we know the future of our students, allowing us to imagine "as if" they may become Nobel Prize winners. Ultimately, it keeps us from succumbing to theocracies—and from creating our own.

REFLECTION

When Dan Hilliard heard about Pullman's "as if," he imagined that by acting "as if" he could teach whatever he wished, despite the expectations of his "theocracy." He hesitated, however, when he realized that making such a decision should only be in the context of an aligned curriculum. Simply teaching what he wanted to would be wrong; he would be creating his own theocracy. Still, he liked Pullman's call to listen to the universe and bring one's own values to the table. He vowed to bring his best to his students every day. He wondered, too, after reading about Eisner's five principles, how he might incorporate them into this teaching.

POINTS TO PURSUE

☑ Which outside ideas have moved you to rethink your teaching? Do you have some you have kept in the wings? Explore them with colleagues to test their viability.

☑ Do you feel pressure from oppressive "theocracies" on your teaching? If so, what might you do to free yourself of them to become the teacher you need to be for your students? How can you seek help from others? If you've overcome such pressures, how were you able to do it? How can you help colleagues do the same?

☑ If you decide to succumb to theocracy, particularly one that you deplore, weigh carefully the consequences on you and your students.

☑ Take Eisner's five principles one at a time and explore their meaning with colleagues. As you come to understand them, implement them in your teaching and observe their effect. Plan to observe each other for feedback.

☑ Look up and apply Marzano's exemplary ten questions, one or two at a time, as you did with Eisner's principles. Discuss what they mean with peers and use them in your teaching.

☑ If we take Pullman's "as if" seriously, it will change our thinking. We will likely alter our internal conversations, those self-communiqués that define who we think we are and can be. Adopting "as if" thinking, we become open to what transpires and to what touches our heart. We become different teachers.

CHAPTER 18

Take the Long View

Being a consultant has provided me with opportunities to live inside the minds and hearts of new teachers. Gathering after school or on Saturday mornings, we discussed the trials, tribulations, and possibilities of being new in this most challenging profession. This letter symbolizes the kind of thinking these new teachers and I have had together.

November 2008

Dear Marie,

I admired your courage and honesty today in our new teachers' class. You shared the woes of your first months and opened others to share theirs. While you may not feel much better, at least you learned that you are not alone.

When you crossed over to the other side of the teacher's desk you quickly discovered more than met your eye as a student. You had watched your teachers glide through lessons year after year, but in taking your turn, you have stumbled and faltered more than you expected. You imagined students would gravitate to your love of learning, but you watched them instead chatter and doze off. You entered your high-school classroom having magic in your heart only to see it quickly fizzle. No wonder you are hurting.

I can't blame you. You decided to teach because you wanted to bond with students in ways only a few teachers did with you. Yet, whatever you have tried has turned out differently. Many of your students reject your enthusiasm, hardly pay attention, slouch at their desks, and rarely do homework. Only a few seem to like what you do.

You told us your department head has observed you only once in the past three months and offered few suggestions, none of which have worked. Your mentor listens to you and suggests alternatives, but has no time in her schedule to spend time in your classroom. You feel alone, deserted with thirty armchair desks full of uninterested students.

What can you do? You might begin by stepping back and take the long view of your life as a teacher. You have already told me you had decided to become a teacher when you sat in Mr. Rowe's tenth-grade science class. You admired his unique manner, his gift of storytelling, and his understanding of the deeper purposes of biology. You saw yourself as like him, and then decided you wanted to teach biology as he has.

Now you are in your own room, but your teaching is not like Mr. Rowe's. I know you are disappointed. But, if you take the long view and visualize putting it all together, you will see you will not become Mr. Rowe, nor should you. Becoming a teacher—a great teacher—takes years (at least ten) of giving one hundred ten percent every day. It is an iterative process that demands commitment, energy, and persistence. I have no doubt from our conversations that you will accept the challenge.

In our class, you have heard some of your colleagues claim to have few difficulties in their classes—or so they say. Their students like them—as your students no doubt like you. A few years ago, I taught a group of new teachers in which a third-grade teacher had no behavioral issues. Her colleagues were in awe, as they were all facing their own challenges. She realized later on she had the luck of the draw, since the next year's third grade proved more challenging.

In our class, we have been discussing ideas and approaches about classroom management, lesson design, and assessment. I realize that only some of the ideas appear workable at this point, as your style and the context of your classrooms seem to limit their applicability. What works for one teacher may not for another. Unfortunately, no recipes for success exist, because teaching combines the science of practice with our personal artistry.

Whenever my teaching appeared topsy-turvy and out of sorts, I often turned to the kaleidoscope metaphor. The colorful glass pieces represented the students, parents, colleagues, administrators, ideas, and concerns swirling about me. The more disconnected, disoriented, and disappointed I felt, the faster the stones seemed to tumble. Some days they would spin so fast that everything blurred. But when I stepped back, I gained more control—at least a better perspective—the pieces slowed and patterns started to emerge. Whenever they came to a stop, I discovered insights, clarity, joy, successes, connections, and epiphanies. Meaning, direction, and purpose showed up. I felt I was where I belonged. I remembered I was doing what I had been called to do.

Such instances may not occur often, especially early in your teaching. Remember, Marie, teaching ultimately is not about what happens *to* us; it's about what we *do*—and *can do* for our students.

Try the kaleidoscope metaphor. When you sense it spinning fast, see it as a message to take time for yourself. Begin to take deep breaths, enjoy a quiet meal, a movie, or a conversation with a friend. Step back to realize you are a young teacher who is in it for the long haul, who knows she can become better and better—and will.

As the tumbling slows, become alert. Look for possibilities as to how to shift gears, to make changes, to discover new paths. Recognize the kaleidoscope as a reflection of your mind and heart as it sorts and clarifies. Sometimes it feels like a mentor. The more open you are the more the kaleidoscope will speak to you.

When the pieces become still, pay close attention to their arrangement. Take advantage of what you are seeing and take time to reflect. Write in your journal; write a letter to yourself or to a colleague; talk into a voice recorder; call a friend or relative. Whatever works for you, take that time. You will solidify your newfound insights and make them part of your practice. After all, we become what we practice.

Remember, Marie, you bring your best teacher self to school every day. Now that you stand on the other side of the teacher's desk, remember to take the long view, and pay attention to what you see in your kaleidoscope.

When you get into your car after school, take a deep breath and tell yourself, "I'm here! I made it through the day!" Reflect upon the good moments; for example, Debbie, a "lost" student, passed in her homework; Mary smiled when she walked in your room; Rebecca, your mentor, told you Joe Roberts (one of your challenging kids) loves your class; and Paul, your principal, complemented you about how you handled a parent conference. Only after such celebrating should you think about what did not go so well. Keep everything in perspective! Keep the long view!

Be well,

Frank

P.S. By the way, remember to buy tickets, so you'll be sure to do something for yourself!

REFLECTION

New teachers face challenges threatening their commitment nearly every day. Given that half of them leave the profession within five years, we need to be cognizant of their need for support, care, and love. Dan Hilliard felt blessed in his early years, as he worked closely with Mel Goodwin, his department chair. In fact, "Mr. Goodwin" and he co-taught during his first three years. As a result, Mel took an interest in Dan's teaching and often observed him and gave feedback. Years after Mel retired, Dan learned that he regarded Dan as the best young teacher in the department. Mel had taught him well.

Fortunately, Dan realized early in his teaching the need to establish personal relationships with his students and their families. Teachers, too, need personal—and professional—relationships with colleagues, if they are to succeed. Too often, new teachers are given heavy caseloads (as veterans prefer "easier groups"), and these teachers are left to their own devices. When new teachers struggle, they are frequently seen as problematic rather than needing help.

Dan discovered Ross Greene's *Lost at School* and decided to implement Greene's Assessment of Lagging Skills and Unsolved Problems (ALSUP) inventory when faced with particularly challenging students.[120] He realized that Greene's approach could benefit his new colleagues who struggled with difficult students. He took time to share Greene's approach with them.

He realized, too, that Greene's ideas applied to all of his students, and more importantly, should be applied throughout the school. He recommended *Lost at School* to his principal as a reading priority for the faculty. He agreed to chair a committee to implement Greene's ideas.

As for Marie, she found the kaleidoscope metaphor to be helpful, but she decided to seek out Dan and ask if he might observe her. She liked his ideas and the direction he was taking with his teaching. She was particularly fascinated with the story of the day he taught from Sam's seat.

POINTS TO PURSUE

☑ If you are a new teacher, what support do you have? What support would you like to have? Can you find a colleague (new or veteran) to whom you can explain your needs?

☑ As a new teacher, make it a point to form close relationships. Plan not only to arrange social engagements, but also schedule regular times to meet to discuss classroom issues. Forming collegial relationships is as important in the long run—perhaps more important—as developing congeniality. (You will find that teachers easily form congenial relationships, but struggle to develop open and honest dialogue about their teaching.)

☑ If you are veteran, have you paid attention to the newer members of the staff? If you are a mentor, have you made time to support your mentee, to "be there" at any time and in any way necessary? If you are colleague and not a mentor, in addition to being friendly, have you offered to observe and help your newer colleagues. Have you attempted to forge a professional relationship with new teachers, as well as a personal one?

☑ Try the kaleidoscope metaphor for your teaching life. Assess how it helps you maintain focus, purpose, and patience. Share your thinking about this idea.

☑ Read Ross Greene, *Lost at School*, to determine its place in your classroom and in your school. It will be time well spent!

CHAPTER 19

Invoke the Cosmos

Some days we find ourselves swirling amid epiphanies, momentary insights, or revealed truths. We see a resistant student suddenly proclaiming her grasp of a concept that had eluded both her and her classmates. We catch a parent recognizing his child's newfound successes. We discover that our principal anticipated our plan to improve our team. These moments also happen in unlikely places, in the middle of the night, in the shower, on a walk, when reading, or simply sitting still.

It happened to me one summer morning at chapel on Star Island. Brian Swimme, cosmologist and chaplain at a conference, shared a discovery by astronomers who had seen a spiral galaxy (a galaxy with one center alive with active stars) coming into contact with an elliptical galaxy (a galaxy with two foci stuck inside itself with no active stars) and bringing it to life![121] I do not remember the rest of Brian's talk, because I was immersed in imagining the idea of teachers as spiral galaxies called to bring life to children.

Swimme's metaphor offers us the chance not only to see ourselves as activating an engaged and curious life but also of knowing and understanding the life we can bring to others. As adults and teachers, we need to know who we are and to become conscious of our mission. We need to accept the realities before us and seek possibilities for transforming them into the greater good. We need, in the words of a colleague, "to be icons of the future possibility of living and empowering life."[122] We can, if we choose, become spiral galaxies and breathe life into our students.

I entered teaching, like many, eager to touch lives. I imagined making a difference to my students, parents and school. Rarely have I had passive days. I have remained alive to what I've taught and have sought the new and different, even when I taught the same subject or grade level year after year. I never burned out. In Swimme's metaphor, I taught as a spiral galaxy, full of life, eager to share and generate creative lives in others. I still do.

Yet, we live in a society that chooses to rear children inside cocoons of endless directed activities, ones that drain them of energy and creativity as they contend with our invasive culture. They appear suspended lifeless between two foci: one in face-to-face relationships to family and friends and the other in a faceless relationship to their electronic "family and friends."

Children have less time to choose, and less time to play and relate to peers as they spend more and more time alone. They shuffle from one activity to another after school and on weekends, and in between spend time before televisions, computers, cell phones electronic games, and the Internet. Arriving in our classrooms, they appear less able to initiate, decide, and inquire. They wait for our direction. They seem uncomfortable in face-to-face encounters, and perhaps feel naked without their electronic devices under their thumbs.

Despite the allure of glitzy new technologies, ironically, our children may be living inside stagnant elliptical galaxies with little or no self-generated energy. I recall Susan Rubenstein's commentary more than ten years ago about her high school English students who claimed that they could not have a discussion at the dinner table because they did not have dinner with their parents.[123] Our latchkey culture has left children and adolescents at home alone; the myriad of electronic technologies only adds to the isolation. Schools lament the listlessness of increasing numbers of obese children who have little desire to participate, to seek, to understand. Classroom teachers notice greater and greater apathy among students. Art teachers in schools and museums express frustration with children's lack of imagination. The image of our children having two foci living inside elliptical galaxies is compelling. In essence, children act as texts without context.

If we choose to act as spiral-galaxy teachers, we can activate energy in our students. When we visualize them as dual-foci beings, we raise our consciousness to look beyond appearances into the real selves before us. When we act as activators towards life, we resonate at the heart of the universe. Human consciousness, as far as we know, is unique among all creatures (at least on this planet) in that we can reflect on our place in the universe. Quantum mechanics teaches us that the act of looking affects what we see—the observer affects the observed. If we choose to look at people and objects as alien life forms, we deny our interconnection. But, we have been born of the same source and exchange atoms with everyone and everything around us.

As teachers, we need to see our students as integral to our lives, as part of the extended human family, as part of the same universe.

Let's look at this another way. Suppose a spiral galaxy and an elliptical galaxy touched, and the reverse happened and the spiral galaxy were to die? Would not the universe be conveying a different message? Instead of affirming life as essential to the universe knowing itself, it would be declaring the opposite. But instead, we are a unique part of a creative universe and as a part we reveal the universe. What happens at the macrocosm level is echoed in the microcosm. As Ken Wilber puts it in *A Brief History of Everything*:

> There's an old joke about a King who goes to a Wiseperson and asks how is it that the Earth doesn't fall down. The Wiseperson replies, "The Earth is resting on a lion." "On what then is the lion resting?" "The lion is resting on an elephant." "On what is the elephant resting?" "The elephant is resting on a turtle." "On what is the. . ." "You can stop right there, Your Majesty, It's turtles all the way down."[124]

The universe favors life. It insists on the emergence of life, otherwise we would not be here. By no means could the universe generate itself as it has in the past 13.5 billion years in random fashion. The universe exudes intelligence. Just how this occurs, we can only surmise, but it appears obvious in the results it has produced thus far. At the same time, we will not survive as a species any more than the Earth will survive when the sun dies in four billion years. Already, ninety-nine percent of all species that ever existed on Earth have become extinct. Yet, clearly life has been an outcome of the particular universe in which we live. Certainly, it does not take up residence exclusively on planet Earth. Life will live beyond our time.

Perhaps, our understanding of who we are begins by acknowledging each of us as a fragment of a greater whole, a single stitch in a garment. As fragments we participate in the life around us, making our contributions and accepting the contributions of others. Each of us emerges unique. As teachers entering our classrooms for the first time, we know we do not replace the previous teacher as a new light bulb replaces a worn light bulb. Instead, we come as unique fragments that have never been here nor ever will be here again.

We are, in Ken Wilber's terminology, holons, simultaneously

whole and part.[125] "Each grain of sand or snowflake is a holon in and of itself. But only in aggregation as a part of the whole does one contribute to the beach or the blizzard."[126] As wholes, we need to act as agents, as active holons in the world embodying the change we want. Or, in the words of Gandhi, "Be the change you wish to see in the world."

At the same time, we need to act in communion. If we do not, we will not survive. As humans, we find meaning in community. Solitary fragments become a shard, brittle and disconnected. When broken off from the whole—obvious when absent in a huge ceramic mosaic—not only will we be isolated but also we will be missed.

Swimme's metaphor may appear grandiose when we compare it to ourselves in our classrooms. Yet, it reminds us of our universe home. It allows us to see our teacher lives as part of the continuum of the Universe Story and in particular, as conduits and creators of human history.

As Wilber said, "It's turtles all the way down."

REFLECTION

When Dan Hilliard heard Carl Sagan lecture on the universe, he suddenly saw himself in its unfolding story. His friends chide him about this perspective, but he won't let it go. Later, he read Brian Swimme and Thomas Berry's *The Universe Story*, and Ken Wilber's *A Brief History of Everything*, which only solidified his convictions. He sees himself as a teacher born of star stuff, taking his turn in human history to responsibly fulfill his—and its—purpose. He knows his purpose resides in his teaching, and he gives himself to it every day.

At the same time, he understands that within this grand microcosm, he must pay attention to what's in front of him. Each student, each colleague, and each grain of sand—each fragment, if you will—counts. Life's fullness requires his fullness.

Dan tries to intrigue colleagues to read and discuss these ideas, but few take any interest. He shares his thoughts in class whenever it seems to fit and finds many of his students curious to know more. One year, he spent six weeks teaching the origin of the universe as an elective. Nearly all of his students were enthralled.

POINTS TO PURSUE

☑ How does the universe story connect to our teaching? What does it mean when a spiral galaxy creates life for an elliptical galaxy? What does it mean that consciousness expands? That we are the universe knowing itself? That the universe really is "turtles all the way down?" What do you think? How wonderful it is to teach inside questions we can at best only surmise! What a treat for the brain to activate its deepest realms in search for understanding our purpose and ourselves!

☑ If you've never considered the universe perspective, read a Carl Sagan book, view him on YouTube, or watch *Cosmos*, the television series that opened people to the universe perspective; or for more recent perspectives read Brian Swimme and Thomas Berry's *The Universe Story*, and Ken Wilber's *A Brief History of Everything*. (For a pithy, up-to-date introduction to *The Universe Story*, view the ten-part "Brian Swimme Video Series" on YouTube.) See what happens to your thinking about teaching. Better yet, find some colleagues to join you. Suspend your disbelief, as you embark.

☑ "Each grain of sand or snowflake is a holon in and of itself. But only in aggregation as a part of the whole does one contribute to the beach or the blizzard." What does this mean to you, and to your teaching?

CHAPTER 20

Imagine the Ideal

More than twenty-five years ago, at a conference of social studies teachers, Fred Jervis, Founder and President of the Center for Constructive Change, asked us, "What is an ideal doorman?" We offered a litany of qualities including: appears well dressed, holds the door, gives smiles, acts efficiently, carries bags, hails a cab quickly, and knows all the neighboring restaurants and their menus. Fred then let us know where he was taking us: "Once you know the characteristics of an ideal doorman and you want to become one, you can then plan backwards to get yourself there."[127]

This is a simple but profound concept, one I have used in my teaching ever since. For example, I once taught a brief unit on Egypt in which my eight graders interviewed second graders who had been studying Egypt as their central subject, and already knew more than my students ever would. Before they began, however, I explained the final outcome: In three weeks, they would complete a mini-book (I showed examples) for their paired second grade student, which they would create by researching books on Egypt in the library. From there, we planned backwards—and it worked well.

Taking a lead from Fred Jervis, what if we imagined that we could teach in our ideal classroom? What would it look like? Sound like? Act like? As I began thinking, I realized, unlike Plato's ideal form, that each classroom would be distinct from the others. Until classrooms cease to exist, they need to become unique and personal.

In *my* ideal classroom, my co-teachers and I create a space with its own story and aura. We might have a few desks and chairs but we also have couches, upholstered chairs, area rugs, plants, curtains, and perhaps a teacher's desk but set off to the side. Students' fine art and stimulating ideas grace the walls. Music plays at in-between times. There is no litter. Students arrive expecting the unexpected, but certain they will learn. Everyone greets each other by name and with a smile. Learning begins the moment we enter and carries on as we leave. There are no bells, and no public address announcements.

As teachers, we evoke deep respect and treat students as honored guests. We accept them as they are and welcome them into to a safe learning place. We teach them to take breaths to center themselves. We help them to bring focus to their work. We teach without stress. We enjoy what we are doing. We enjoy each and every one of our students.

We ask more questions and give fewer answers. We create conversations using reason, evidence, and temperance. We invoke empathy, encourage different viewpoints, and expect rigor. We believe each student can and will learn and do anything to make it happen. We concentrate on what they do well, and nurture their weaknesses through their strengths to help them gain confidence and thrive. We value thinking and take time to give students' brains opportunities to ponder, explore, and consider. We value the struggle needed to develop worthwhile insights.

We work. Productive, useful, thoughtful, attentive, honest, and persistent work. Purpose is evident everywhere. Rigor means striving without fear of judgment. We provide frequent and consistent feedback during the learning process. We transform failures into successes. Teaching and learning become everyone's business. Students learn to teach themselves.

We strive to answer the question, "What's worth knowing?" even though we do not know what jobs await our students, or what technologies, or what problems they will face. We take responsibility, to teach tools for lifelong learning as best as we know how.

We build a culture of creativity, a culture of innovation. We resist making academics the sole concentration, and instead build learning around all facets of intellectual and emotional learning. Students have equal access to the arts, humanities, and sciences and understand they have equal value in their learning lexicon.

We allow the work to become evidence for learning. The quality of students' work reflects the quality of our teaching. We strive to provide authentic performance assessment opportunities. We do not grade students against each other, but instead provide honest, summative assessments of their progress in relationship to clear goals and standards.

We use technology, including smart boards, overheads, VCR/DVDs, computers, cell phones, iPods, and the Internet. Online learning is central, giving students opportunities to use familiar resources in a framework of sensible thinking, reading, writing, discussion, and creative media and arts. We remain open to emerging technologies and their possibilities to enhance learning. We value face-to-face encounters and do not allow technological interactions to supercede them. We spend long periods of time without electronic distractions to build habits of concentration and deep thinking. And we treasure humanity's uniqueness, its gift to itself, by learning together through love, laughter, sharing, cajoling, reading, writing, discussing, engaging, playing, eating, walking together, and so on.

We provide equal opportunities for learning—and insist everyone can learn and does. We move on to new learning together only when everyone demonstrates that they are ready. Teaching means to invite, as invitation is our best motivator.

We build relationships to create a culture of appreciation. Our ideal classroom invites its own sacredness, its reason for being. It acts as a tribe, so to speak, sharing rituals, mythology, and culture. It lives beyond the school day—everyone feels free to stay connected, ask for help, and share learning in person, by phone, or online.

We are present to everyone and everything. We listen. My colleagues and I are never satisfied and are always seeking the next-best way to making learning happen for our students and for us.

I enjoy pondering the ideal classroom. Of course, yours will undoubtedly be different. Nevertheless, visualizing the ideal helps us align priorities and awaken possibilities. I sense most of us do not take time, however, as we have so much to do. Yet, when I walk through hallways and see countless rooms with desks in rows and columns, I wonder why so many of us persist to teach in this way. I come back to these familiar, persistent questions:

What keeps us boxed in?
What keeps us replicating the ways of our predecessors?
What prevents us from letting go of convention and seeking the ideal?
How can we ignore the presence of the future and not feel its energy pulling us to reform our teaching practices?

Such questions are not about blame but about curiosity. If we neglect to ponder the ideal, we may remain unconscious of the precious delight inherent in teaching. In the 1970s, open education inspired alternative settings. My classroom included areas for reading, cooking, drama, music, painting, illustrating, science, math, writing, calligraphy—and a bicycle repair shop. Colorful fabrics divided spaces and student artwork and calligraphy hung on the walls. Three of us co-taught all subjects side-by-side. We nurtured students to use planbooks to organize and self-assess their learning. We taught in this way less than ten years, then the powers-at-be absorbed us into a traditional middle school.

Perhaps when we decide to teach in a way that makes it possible for each and every student to learn, we will break out of the mold of the "regular classroom." When we move to teach from the middle of the room, we discover and create new patterns and new ways to interact and relate. We establish our own identity, which is the genesis of our ideal classroom.

Building our ideal classroom from the bottom—a curious idea! We can do it if we imagine. One ideal at a time.

REFLECTION

Once teachers begin to move away from the front, possibilities for learning appear. As Dan Hilliard tried more active strategies, he saw his classroom as unique. He wondered what his ideal classroom might look like. He began to think about removing desks, bringing in plants, expanding beyond academics, putting questions first, and more.

In evoking the ideal, Dan realized, too, he needed to be real. He did not want to be gimmicky for gimmick's sake. Seeking the ideal demands rigor—and intention, direction, unity, and sequence, at a minimum.

He asked to have a faculty meeting devoted to considering "the ideal." He wondered how his colleagues would react. After some thought, he realized "the ideal" could apply to a subject area, a department, a grade level, and not only to a classroom. His principal agreed to devote a meeting to "the ideal," but asked teachers to help him plan it. He did not want to impose it as his agenda but wanted buy in from everyone. Dan liked this approach.

POINTS TO PURSUE

☑ When we imagine the ideal in any aspect of our teaching, we begin to think of exciting alternatives. We start to see in a new light. We might approach a new unit in an unusual way, or begin by circling desks around the edge of the room. What would be the purpose of such an arrangement? Where would you sit? What would happen in the middle? Where to next?

☑ Imagine tossing out the textbook (if you haven't already). How would students react? How would students get material? What would they do for homework?

☑ Gather some colleagues and ask the question: "How can we create classrooms to stimulate learning instead of passivity?" Observe what they generate.

☑ What happens when you remove grading from the equation of teaching?

☑ Find the teachers who students and parents love. Visit them to learn their secrets. You might find elements for your ideal classroom. You might find a new colleague.

PART V

How Do We Find Our Calling?

Ultimately, successful teaching requires understanding who we are and what we want. Unless we take time to seek our inner teacher, we deny ourselves the deep richness that teaching can bring to us and to the lives of our students, their families, and our colleagues. "Know thyself," proclaimed Socrates, who also said, "An unexamined life is not worth living." Attending to our personal and spiritual growth is essential.

We need to recognize, first, the nature of our calling. Each of us takes our own path to decide to teach and become the teacher we are. We also need to pay attention to the practices we implement, determine their effectiveness, and only choose to keep those that work. We need to periodically reexamine our philosophy and the nature of our journey, as we learn to become the chief stakeholders in our teaching. We need, too, to articulate for ourselves and for our students the knowledge, understandings, and skills we intend to teach.

Finally, we need to recognize the crucial role we have in the successes (and failures) of our students and the differences we make. We need to believe in the honor that teaching bestows upon us, and work towards realizing our potential in serving our students, their families, and the community.

CHAPTER 21

Grow Our Seeds

Hardly a day passes when I am not reminded that I have been called to teach, whether in classrooms with students or now with teachers. My classrooms have always been a joy. Something unexplainable happens. My relationships with students, their families, and colleagues create infinite possibilities. I have been blessed every day to learn as much and often more than my students.

James Hillman's "acorn theory" explains it best: ". . . each person bears a uniqueness that asks to be lived and that is already present before it can be lived."[128] As each acorn emerges into its own oak, so does each human emerge into its being. Identical twins are no exception. I connect with Hillman's acorn because I have seen the uniqueness of each child I've taught. While I do not subscribe to his concept of "daimon," or guardian angel (which he insists guides and directs us), I agree with him that we do have a calling—and events align to make it happen.

How can we know if teaching has called us? We feel it when we wake up with yet another idea and rush to write it down. We know it when we see a student suddenly grasp the concept of surface tension while watching a wiper blade move across a windshield.[129] Ursula Boyle knew it when she decided to spend twice the required hours for a course writing, reflecting, and responding. Jenn Drew and Leighann Wright sensed it when they decided to take a course not for credit or professional development, but because they wanted to learn so they could share their learning with colleagues; I felt it whenever the bell rang after ninety minutes of conversation with my eighth graders, wondering where the time went; my students and I had become so immersed in our learning. We rediscover our calling in myriads of ways.

We feel a persistent passion, and sense the sacred in everything. We ask questions with a child's curiosity. We make a cup of coffee for the pleasure of making a cup of coffee. We pound a nail with joy knowing what we are building. We serve others with delight as if we were our own customers. We teach as if we are our students. Each act has meaning. Each act belongs.

When we understand that we are our own seed growing into who we are, we become open to the unexpected. It happened for me when Gorbachev's perestroika lured me to the Soviet Union. I had been living and breathing Marxism, Communism, the Soviets, and everything Russian since my second-year of teaching. The more my students and I explored the Soviets, the more I tried to reconcile the Soviet public face with what I believed lurked behind the scenes. The combination of Gorbachev's ascension in March 1985, and the ability of Bridges for Peace, a local community group, to facilitate Soviet-American exchanges gave me an opportunity to see for myself. My first trip followed that October.

I would have shaken my head in disbelief had someone told me then that I would later travel to the Soviet Union and Russia eight times—three times as a teacher in Soviet schools! Fifteen years earlier, I had traveled to Oxfordshire, England, with my wife and two children, hoping to find a job in a progressive primary school, which I did. But that was more predictable, given my study of British primary education in graduate school the year before. With no Slavic heritage, I wondered why I felt compelled to travel and teach in the Soviet Union.

Why did these Soviet experiences pan out while others did not? Why did my teaching about the Soviets become three-dimensional when other wishes and dreams at that time never materialized? Why was my first trip practically a red carpet spread before me? Other "callings" I assumed were mine did not happen. The most obvious was my wish to become a principal. No matter when or where I applied, I either did not have the right résumé, or came in second or third, or chose not to accept a position offered. Upon reflection, the old cliché, "it was never meant to be" seems applicable.

When we think back to our childhoods, we remember what attracted us, what pulled us in, what invited our curiosity. As we move through life, we meet people who slip into our web as if they had always been there, while others do not find a home with us. We find that we like some things and dislike others, often with no apparent reason. We care passionately about some issues and ignore others, while our friends may do the opposite. We become obsessed with baseball or dolls or video games, or in the case of my grandson, Jon, before he was two years old, vacuum cleaners! We live with these obsessions as if they are directly connected to us, as if they called us. Why we do this is a mystery.

We have nondescript moments (at the time) that linger. I remember one such moment when I was about ten years old. I was standing on a sidewalk on Spring Street when I saw my father, who was a college administrator, across the street talking with Jimmy Donahue. I was taken aback because my friends (and everyone else it seemed) believed that Jimmy was different, and for lack of a better term, slow. He dressed in tattered suits and had a speech defect. Sometimes, we would mock him behind his back.

At home, I asked my father why he took time to talk with Jimmy. He told me that everyone is worth talking to. This moment stuck with me. I know I have not always followed his words, as I can get caught up in paying special attention to "important" people. Yet, I believe differently. Among the "important" people in my life are not only professors, teachers, shop owners, lawyers, and city officials, but also postal clerks, garage attendants, janitors, cooks, and street cleaners; I know their names and many of their stories.

Do the memories we keep, such my memory of my father, instruct us toward our own calling? Are they fertilizer for our seeds? Do we see them because they have been placed before us? I have another Soviet story that speaks to this. It was an afternoon some twenty years ago at the massive Palace of Pioneers in Moscow, the showcase of the city's chosen Young Pioneers. In their blue uniforms with red scarves, these children performed in multiple glass-encased rooms for thousands of visitors from around the world. I stood alone, however, gazing through a door into a large, nearly empty room. A Young Pioneer girl stood in the near corner all by herself, playing school with dolls at miniature desks. I was mesmerized as I watched her teach her dolls. Tourists raced up and down the stairs behind me.

The child revealed a curious intensity as she stood in front of her "children," directing them with attentive, quizzical, and sometimes scowling looks. She put herself in charge, no doubt about it. She never saw me. I wonder if this child ever became a teacher. She had internalized the demeanor of Soviet teachers with whom I had worked. A sense of purpose. Devotion. Control. Parental posture. A Soviet teacher, after all, served as a surrogate parent for the state and assumed full responsibility for the patriotic character of her students.

In the end, I do not think the way this Moscow child, or any child, plays school matters much. What matters was that her *desire* to play school—a hint of a calling perhaps—revealed more than the act itself. This Young Pioneer, a product of a conformist culture, appeared to be nurturing her own seed by choosing what she wanted to do without pretense, for her own satisfaction and no one else's. At least that's the way I saw it.

REFLECTION

Dan Hilliard recalls his sophomore year in college when he was hired to take care of thirty children of alumni attending their twenty-fifth reunion. It was then he realized his desire to become a teacher. It was the first time he had been given responsibility without having to do someone else's bidding; he needed to keep the children safe and happy, and how he did it was up to him.

By the time he stepped into his first classroom, he knew he belonged. He's never doubted it since. He knows colleagues who also have a strong sense of their calling. They seem more confident and more flexible—more willing to move their teaching into the middle of the room.

POINTS TO PURSUE

☑ Do you agree with Hillman's acorn metaphor "... that each person bears a uniqueness that asks to be lived and that is already present before it can be lived?" Have you sensed the uniqueness of your teaching; that is, that you are unlike any teacher before you, around you, or who will come after you? If you have not, take time to reflect on your special attributes and find ways to celebrate who you are.

☑ Do these words from John Updike appeal to you: "There's a kind of confessional impulse that not every literate, intelligent person has ... a crazy belief that you have some exciting news about being alive ... what separates those who do it from those who think they'd like to do it. That your witness to the universe can't be duplicated, that only you can provide it, and that it's worth providing."[130] Are you willing to see "that your witness to the universe can't be duplicated"? Are you willing to see yourself as unique, special, a one-of-a-kind?

☑ What events have become seminal in your life? How have they helped to define you? How do they define you as a teacher?

☑ What if we provide more time for students in all grades to play in the classroom? Would we learn more about who they are, as in the story of the Young Pioneer in the Moscow Palace? Would they learn more about who they are, what they value, and what they want in life? What can we do to justify play when we are pressured to apply more time on task?

CHAPTER 22

Empty the Black Bag

When I first conceived this book, I imagined writing in the third person and pointing fingers at my fellow teachers. I formed my argument around the metaphor of emptying the country doctor's black bag. I cited the medical profession's decision in the early twentieth century to empty its black bag of old fashioned instruments, then patent medicines and establish and monitor standards. I contrasted this with the teaching profession's reluctance to do the same, instead continuing to use traditional practices and pedagogies while failing to invoke standards.[131] *Emptying the Black Bag: Giving Children What They Deserve* was this book's original title.

But, I soon realized this metaphor encompassed only part of the picture, as the quality of teaching has never been about prescribing high standards and implementing the right methodology. If true, we would only need to find the right formulas and apply them. But, were we to do so, what would be missing? Would lessons be meaningful? Would implementing them fulfill our calling? Certainly not. Research confirms that successful teaching focuses on results—what students learn—not on specific pedagogies. As Robert Marzano concludes, "There is no right way to teach."[132]

Returning to the black bag metaphor, I do not advocate discarding the contents of traditional teaching simply because they are old. Certainly, doctors replacing antique medical instruments with modern equipment made obvious sense, just as schools have replaced desks bolted to the floor with movable furniture. But, the metaphor elicits deeper meaning beyond tools and procedures. It's about who we are and who we need to be.

Let me begin from the medical point of view, with the story of a doctor from my early life.

The first doctor's black bag in my life belonged to Norman B. McWilliams, our soft-spoken, mustached family doctor who brought it with him during house calls. Dr. Mac used many of the same instruments in his comfortable office, with its fuzzy green-felt outer door, located over the National Bank. Being around him, I felt reassured, as his voice was soothing and calm. And he and his wife Isabel frequently came to our home as family friends.

Dr. Mac no doubt kept up with changes in medical practice, as he always seemed to respond well when we were sick and knew when to pass us onto specialists. But, he never lost his gentle bedside manner, a quality we look for in our doctors today. He reassured us particularly when my mother faced a challenging illness.

While I do not remember the specific tools, procedures, and medicines Dr. Mac discarded, I do know he never let go of his compassionate manner. When we as teachers decide to empty our black bag of outmoded practices, we, too, need to continue to use our good tools and to keep our compassion, our sense of community, and our dedication.

But, once we acknowledge the need to change, we invoke the question, "What do I need to do every day to make meaningful learning happen for each and every student in my classroom?" We know our teaching habits live deep within us, since we learned them well while watching our own teachers. In my last years of teaching in the classroom, for example, I remember hesitating when Chris Boone, our thoughtful middle school head, requested that our eighth-grade team commit to a second meeting in his office each week.[133] We were concerned because it would take away from our personal planning time. Despite the appeal of more collaboration and the obvious benefit for students, my colleagues and I indicated our preference to keep our old ways. We did not prevail, however, despite insisting that our planning periods were essential—and in many schools would have been protected in union contracts. We quickly discovered that the second meeting proved invaluable.

Perhaps you, too, had a epiphany while hearing Randy Pausch's speech at Carnegie Mellon; when he posted his "Last Lecture" on YouTube, he had an inoperable cancer with only six-months to live.[134] His stories and insights riveted listeners. His wisdom touched everyone. He spoke as if he had ascended a mountaintop, found wisdom, and came back to share it. As I listened, I wondered how many of us have such wisdom within us ready to be tapped. Does the threat of impending death, of an approaching end awaken us to what we know? Or, does this threat awaken us as listeners to be open to such wisdom from people like Randy before they leave us?

In the spirit of Einstein's thought problems:

What if we imagined we had only six months left to teach?

What if we saw these six months as *the* opportunity to teach as we have always wanted to teach?

Would we discover our own wisdom and feel compelled to share it with our colleagues and students?

Would we become free to teach as our real selves rather than feeling we must fulfill the expectations of others?

Could we actually evoke this sense of urgency?

It would be a challenge to pretend we have "only six months left" to teach. We naturally believe we will have next year, and the next, and the next, until retirement. Yet, we can recognize that we have only six months or a year with every class before they move on. We need to find ways to awaken to every minute and teach to make a real difference.

We can begin by feeling the pressure (or freedom) that constraints play in our lives and our teaching, such as having to meet deadlines. Constraints provide borders to guide our decisions and keep us focused on what we need to do. Without them, we often lose our place.

When we create constraints in the classroom, students gain a clearer sense of what they need to know, understand, and be able to do. I remember a great shift in the quality of work with self-hardening clay in my open classroom after I established straightforward and clear procedures for how to work in the clay bay. First, students could only use enough clay to fit in one hand. Second, they could not make a recognizable object, such as a cup or animal. And lastly, their abstract shape had to have at least one hole.

The result was a series of remarkable sculptures, which led to the discovery of a faux glaze, when the students rubbed the sculptures with polished rocks. The students did this while sitting quietly or listening to stories. Unwittingly, we found a way to build meditation practice into the classroom.

Teaching with the constraint of "only six months left" invites us to see our purpose more clearly. In my final year as a classroom teacher—particularly the last six months!—I became conscious of my presence in school; aware that soon I would no longer have a classroom in which my eighth graders and I could sit in a circle to have deep conversations. Sometimes, I caught myself saying words for the last time. I felt an impending loss when we "published" our last booklet on Eastern Wisdom. I realized as the year came to a close that my legacy would be in my students, and not in the school. In fact, within a couple of years the last building in which I taught was torn down.

I wonder if my teaching career would have been different if I understood I had "only six months left" for each class, each year:

Would I have emptied my own black bag of ineffective practices more quickly?

Would I have been more alert to what I taught and to what my students were actually learning?

Would I have built closer relationships with colleagues?

Would I have been more courageous about doing what I believed?

Would I have been a different teacher?

Would I have been a better teacher?

As I ponder these and other questions about my teaching and myself, I have reached a few conclusions. I certainly would have had a heightened awareness about who I am, why I teach, and what I bring to the classroom. I would have paid more attention to my students as I spoke—and as I listened. I could have been more reflective and fully present. By seeking to discover my inner knowing (within all of us), I would have brought it to the surface earlier than I did.

Though I took advantage of my freedom to create units of study and made them imaginative and interesting, I wish I had paid more attention to how each and every student responded. I had a tendency to become carried away with the novelty of my ideas without attending to their impact on each student. As long as many seemed to be on board, I was happy.

I would have paid more attention to how each student learned. In my early years, I delivered academic knowledge and skills and entertained as much as possible. And, as with my colleagues, I based my assessments on quizzes, tests and papers; the best grades belonged to the "bright" students and lower grades to the "less able." While I later realized the error of my ways, I still did not pay close enough attention to how each student learned and to my part in the process. I wish I had learned sooner about learning styles so I could have diversified my teaching to meet the needs of different types of learners.

I wish I could have had access to the recent research on brain-based learning and the innovative methods and approaches now available to teachers, especially the emphasis on collaborative planning and teaching as exemplified in the professional learning community initiatives. I experienced glimpses of these ideas, but, alas, they were not in place in my time.

I wish I had the courage to have graded papers without names.

Whether or not we are willing to think of our teaching as if it were our last six months, the invitation to change from teaching as talking to teaching for learning remains on the table. Yet, as I have said, we will change only when we decide to. When I first envisioned fellow teachers emptying the black bag of outmoded practices, I saw them replacing them with new methods to cause learning. But, we are more than teachers of significant content, skills, and pedagogies.

Parker Palmer frames it best: "We teach who we are."[135] We first bring our self-knowing into our classrooms, and only from there do we choose our practices. What we do, after all, begins with our intention. In words often attributed to Buddhists including the Dalai Lama, "everything rests on the tip of intention." Teaching is, after all, an intentional activity. Our intentions guide us whether we are aware of them or not. If we decide, then, to make it our intention to shift our teaching from the front into the middle of the room, we will begin to take the necessary steps. If we intend to spend more time alongside our students rather than in front of them, we will find ways to do so.

If any of us still doubts the need to create a sense of urgency to change our teaching, perhaps this anecdote will convince:

> I was waiting in the reception room at the eye surgeon's office for a ride home when I happened to observe a local-access television program with a school superintendent and three high school students.

For nearly a half-hour, the superintendent and students exchanged laudatory comments about the qualities of their high school. The students made comments, as the superintendent nodded, including, "Our campus is better than some colleges"; "We have the most professional TV studio of any school"; "Our school is better equipped than many universities." It was almost as if the program had been scripted.

Then, one girl said, "Given that we have ninety-minute class blocks, I wish we did not have to take notes for the entire time."

The superintendent did not blink.

The DNA of teaching-as-talking not only resides deep in the classroom but also runs through the system from top to bottom.

This is the way it is—what Michael Schmoker calls "the brutal facts."[136] We can choose to respond or not. We know all is not well in our schools. We know all is not well in the country, on the planet. We do not need to wait for someone to tell us to find meaning in our work or to empty our black bags of outmoded practices. We can take steps on our own to teach from the middle of the room. As the Taoists profess, a journey of a thousand miles begins with the first step. Whatever moves we make towards the middle of the room will lead to deeper satisfaction in the work we do with students. Taking those steps requires courage—and support.

REFLECTION

Dan Hilliard has listened to discussions comparing the medical profession's practices compared to teaching. He is embarrassed that the teaching profession has been lax in enforcing standards. He wishes that the current tenure system (three years and you're in) was a thing of the past, and instead, teachers would need to be recertified to maintain their credentials. He has decided to pursue National Board Certification from the National Board for Professional Teaching Standards (NBPTS).[137] He knows it will be challenging, but it will provide him with knowledge and understanding of the latest and best practices.

He knows some of his colleagues teach less well. He feels for students who get "stuck" with those teachers who use old lecture notes, who work by the clock, and who take little interest in the personal lives of their students. Until higher standards for all teachers become mandatory—as they are for other professions—such teachers will be allowed to keep renewing their contracts. There's nothing worse, Dan thinks, than teachers who count the days until retirement—and act that way.

POINTS TO PURSUE

☑   What do you think of the comparison between doctors and teachers? Do you think it's fair for books like Michael Schmoker's *Results Now* to criticize the lack of enforceable standards in our profession? Is it, in part, a matter of money?

☑   If you've not seen it, take time to watch Randy Pausch's video, "The Last Lecture," or read his book, *The Last Lecture*. His freshness, vigor, and sense of humor offers wisdom to remind us how we need to be with our students and their families. Beyond that, his message is provocative, encouraging, and uplifting. Once you've seen it, try out the "only-six-months-left-to-teach" idea with your students. See what happens.

☑   Have you considered the power of intentions as expressed by the Dali Lama? Are you aware of yours, every day, and in every lesson? Choose one area of your teaching you'd most like to change: set your intention, then observe the transition. Invite a colleague to observe and support you.

CHAPTER 23

Rethink Our Philosophy

"Your assignment for the next class will be to write a two-page philosophy of education," said Professor Reggie Archambault, six weeks into our graduate philosophy of education class. How ironic to have been asked to write our educational philosophy before we had taught our first lesson! And only two pages! I chose to lean on the wisdom of Plato, Whitehead, Black, and Dewey, rather than what I thought I knew. How many of us ever choose to write another philosophy of education paper? Not until I had been teaching thirty-five years did I write another one. I regret I did not do it more often.

I'm not sure what spurred me to write another philosophy statement. Perhaps it was because it was my last year in the classroom, and I wanted to clarify my own understandings of teaching. Perhaps it was an effort to make sense of my values and concerns. Perhaps I was curious about what I would say. For whatever the reasons, I found the exercise intriguing, insightful, and self-revealing.

As I wrote, I realized that the core of my beliefs and values came from my life and work, rather than from the wisdom of others. I was surprised at first at my focus on practice. Once written, however, I understood myself better and realized what I bring—and needed to bring—to my students. Had I taken time to write a philosophy at different times throughout my career, I am sure I would have had a clearer focus on the qualities—and deficits—of my teaching, and what to do to improve. I certainly would have developed a stronger self-awareness.

How can we take time to look within when we are busy facing overwhelming demands that we seem never able to overcome? Papers pile up, grades become due, supplies need replenishing, deadlines have to be met, and meetings and conferences add to our workload, let alone the demands of our personal lives. Where will we find time and space to commit to write and share our philosophies of education? What if we do not consider ourselves writers? Why should we bother, anyway?

Here's an idea: Why not make a commitment with some colleagues to rewrite your philosophies, and then agree to meet and share them? Suspend your disbelief (if you have it) and be open to what might come. Establish guidelines to encourage participation, such as:

- Agree to write two pages or less.
- Focus on what you do first, then on what you believe and value.
- Provide concrete details to explain your thinking.
- Set a meeting time to share.
- Agree to meet again to re-examine/revise your philosophies based on your practice.

Setting down core beliefs, however, can be intimidating, particularly if you've never done it. Making a commitment is the first step: actually doing it is the next. The following prompts will help you find points of entry. Try one or two. Once you begin you will tap into your real teacher self. When you share it, you will come even closer. Use these prompts and plunge ahead!

When I first taught, I believed . . . but now . . .

Students used to . . . but now they seem . . .

I used to teach only whole-class lessons, but now . . .

From the first day, I believe I . . . and now I still do . . .

While I still average grades, I value work done later in the term more because . . .

I am struggling with the idea of including cell phones and iPods in my teaching . . .

I found being alone in my classroom hard at first, but now I like it . . .

I used to like being alone in my classroom, but now . . .

Compared to my first years, I learn more and share more with colleagues . . .

It's not as much about what I teach, but rather I am a teacher who . . .

Assigning homework has become a challenge . . .

Sometimes, I wonder if I have a life outside teaching . . .

I feel pressure to meet state tests, so I cannot teach the way I want . . .

I read . . . and it changed my teaching . . .

Here are two statements of philosophy I wrote late in my career. Read them to help you formulate your own statements, or to stimulate discussion.

Statement of Philosophy, February 1998

Worcester, Massachusetts

Paying attention. After years of contemplating, reading, and discussing, I have come to the conclusion my philosophy of life and teaching is about paying attention. Paying attention allows me to be in the present. When I listen without distraction, without preoccupation, without thinking of the next appointment, I become a part of those around me. When a student asks a question and I listen, I can answer with a chance for meaning. Otherwise, our words pass by, each of us soon without a memory of the conversation.

Once during a sitting meditation, I noticed Karl, who reappeared after several months' absence. I knew he had moved to Vermont in part because he was not well. I did not know much more. After the meditation, I felt called to sit on the floor close to him to ask what he was going through. I listened. In the end I learned of his illness and fear. Usually I listen and wait for my turn to share. This time I simply listened.

I think philosophy at its best is practical. What one does becomes one's philosophy. I remember the challenge in graduate school of writing a two-page statement of my philosophy of education. I wish I could find it and see what I said. I remember it was full of platitudes reflecting my love of Dewey, Black and Whitehead. I remember, too, typing it on erasable paper on my tiny Royal typewriter. Since then, however, my educational philosophy has become entwined with my life. I find no separation between my practice at work, at home, and on the street. It's the challenge of living a good life, a caring life—and it meets me everywhere.

Showing up. Sometimes that's all it takes. Being there. Being there means to be fully present to others. It is not simply putting in an appearance, but being a presence. The best days in school are those where I am in the midst of it all, an integral part of the swirl. Whether leading a discussion, sharing a pun, observing a colleague, listening to a parent, complimenting the kitchen help, thanking a friend . . . whenever I am attentive to where I am it makes all the difference.

I like details. I like setting up my chairs for the incoming class. I like copying and collating a test or a handout. I like cleaning the table after having lunch with my advisees. I like saying "thank you" and enjoy finding opportunities to say it. I like writing comments to parents about their children. I like the business of life. Doing it well makes possible doing it well again. It's habit.

I read a lot. Aldous Huxley, Fred Alan Wolf, Jon Kabat-Zinn, Lao-tzu, Thich Nhat Hanh, The Dali Lama, Ken Wilber, Brian Swimme, Annie Dillard, and others. I like entering others' minds and trying to understand their perspective. Wilber's *A Brief History of Everything* does it in a big way. I like to invite my students to be writers, particularly about provocative, challenging subjects. I then can read their insights, which frequently touch me deeply.

I enjoy seeking meaning. Besides reading, I attend services and Transformations, a weekly spirituality discussion group at our Unitarian Church. I like the collective search process, which includes all paths. It requires attention and gentle speaking. I also attend a weekly Buddhist meditation group and attempt some meditation on my own with varying success. Seeking in silence is often rich, particularly for one who likes to talk.

I connect with movies as well. I am torn by the increasingly powerful allure films have on all of us. Yet, I can be taken in, sometimes deeply. *Babe* and *Benny and Joon* grabbed me, as did *The Piano*, *Wings of the Dove*, and *Kundun*. I know others will soon do the same, as I will continue to watch both on the big screen and at home. David Attenborough's *Gandhi* was a seminal experience and changed my life. *Close Encounters of the Third Kind* connected me with the universe in a magical way, as did *It's a Wonderful Life* with the power of spirit. I also attend art openings with my wife who is a fine, fine artist. An interesting world. Another perspective, another understanding. And of course, there are plays, concerts, and lectures. They, too, provide doorways.

Doorways can lead to bridges. Bridges provide a context for connecting. I thrive being on a bridge, building understandings and creating resolutions. A bridge can be a safe place to see into one another's worlds, to explore ideas, to encourage empathy, to resolve conflicts. That's why I taught in Russia and the former Soviet Union during glasnost. Meeting others halfway opens creative possibilities and invites reconciliation. And a richer understanding of others—and of myself.

I prefer to work on the edge. I think I have always been this way. Most recently, when asked to teach Ancient history in the eighth grade (having taught Russian and Chinese history for five years), I decided to begin with the Big Bang. After all, why begin at Mesopotamia when civilization was already in place, such a recent event in cosmic time? By seeking the origins of the universe, I wanted to venture into understanding the arrival and meaning of human consciousness. Then, the study of early peoples might make more sense. After two years, I am not sure it does. But it has been fun! And, it is on the edge—Ancient History, after all, is not supposed to begin with the Big Bang.

I like being a messenger. Several years ago, I created what I call wisdom beads, colored pony beads into which I inserted rolled sayings. I began by taking quotations from Thich Nhat Hanh's writings. On the day before winter break, I invite my students each to take a bead from a bowl with the understanding to pay attention to its particular message. We then share them. I also have a set I share with the faculty and staff. This year for the first time, I made some beads for the children in church using my own sayings.

In the end the focus is commitment. A commitment to be of service to others—to do whatever it takes for children, for parents, for colleagues, for the school, for the community. Our commitment must combine competence and excellence, rigorous attention to relationships, and a sense of the awesome responsibility of the profession.

Five years later, I rewrote my philosophy in response to a request as part of a job application. While similar to what I wrote five years earlier, it shows how time and context can reframe our thinking. As in reading a book again after several years, it becomes a new experience. Shades and nuance count.

Statement of Philosophy, April 2003

Worcester, Massachusetts

When I wrote my first philosophy of education statement in graduate school, I remember relying on the wisdom of Alfred North Whitehead, Eugene Black and John Dewey. My statement was idealistic and generalized. As a teacher, I have come to understand my educational philosophy has been only as good as my practice. One of my earliest decisions was to jettison my teacher self and simply try to be me with my students and colleagues. Throughout my years, I have worked to integrate my beliefs about teaching and learning and to close the gap between what I expect from myself and what I accomplish. I now find less and less separation in the practice of my life in my work, at home, and on the street.

My practice begins by listening. Schools are social institutions replete with shifting contexts. Listening allows for presence and for paying attention. When paying attention, we hear what people have to say. When paying attention, we are able to understand thoughts and feelings and to enter into people's lives. When listening without distraction, without preoccupation and without thinking of what we want to say, we become a part of those around us. Whenever a person speaks and we choose to listen, we can respond thoughtfully. Otherwise, our words will pass without memory. When we choose not to listen, people tend to hold their ground and cling to whatever they believe. They are not free to let go and explore.

My practice also means to show up. Sometimes that's all it takes: being there, fully present to others and not simply putting in an appearance. My best days teaching have been when I am in the midst of it all, an integral part of the swirl leading a discussion, observing a colleague, listening to a parent, complimenting a cook, sharing a pun, or thanking a friend. Whenever I am attentive, it makes all the difference.

It means to pay attention to details. Good intentions succeed in the details. Whether making the classroom right for a particular lesson; copying and collating materials; cleaning up after class; smiling at a passerby; listening to a troubled colleague, returning a phone call or email; picking up papers off the floor; or expressing thanks. I enjoy doing the daily business of life.

It means being open to others. I am always seeking meaning. From people and books, from movies, from radio and television, from everywhere. I like to enter the minds of others and to try to understand their perspectives—from Lao-tzu to Ken Wilber, from Jon Kabat-Zinn to Grant Wiggins. As a teacher, I provoke students whenever I can to invite them to share their insights, which often touch me deeply. The teachers with whom I work—veterans and beginners—often startle me when they share their ideas, questions, and understandings. I have learned that wisdom comes in many guises, and I am grateful for every time I recognize it—and wonder how often I miss it.

It means to practice gratitude. In a profession low on prestige and pay, teachers have every reason to resent the lack of respect and support for their efforts. So much of what teachers do happens alone, without notice, without acknowledgment. Yet, I have come to understand the gifts of teaching and its inherent rewards. I have learned to have gratitude for being able to do what I love every day. Gratitude to make a difference in the lives of children, parents, and colleagues. Gratitude to learn every day. And, gratitude to be me, to develop trust in myself, as well as an appreciation for those around me.

It means willing to stand on bridges. Bridges provide a context for connecting, where I can see all sides and participate with all parties. A bridge is a safe place from which to comprehend other worlds, to explore ideas, to encourage empathy, to resolve conflicts. When teaching in the Soviet Union during glasnost, I was on a bridge. Meeting others halfway opens creative possibilities and invites reconciliation, and allows for a richer understanding of others—and of myself.

My philosophy recognizes we are all messengers. We are not always in charge of what we do and how we affect others. Whether we admit it or not, we are often conduits for purposes beyond our comprehension. How many times have others spoken meaning into our lives without their knowing it? How often have we done the same? Most likely we will never know how we touch others' lives. But whenever we find out, we are surprised and delighted. Once in awhile, a letter arrives and tells us we have made a difference. And sometimes we choose to send one. When I ask new teachers to take time to write a letter to someone who made a difference in their decision to be a teacher, they do not hesitate. Education, after all, is a spiritual practice.

Ultimately, my educational philosophy means commitment, a commitment to be in service of others. It means to be willing to do whatever it takes for children and parents, for colleagues and the school, and for the greater community.

And, finally . . .

My Philosophy Reconsidered, 2009

It's been ten years since I last sat with my eight graders. On that last day, the last class, we were sitting in a circle as usual, discussing what, I can't remember, when suddenly we realized we were late for the final middle school assembly.

Arriving late, no one seemed to mind. Neither did Chris Boone, our Head. What a way to leave the classroom for the last time, I said to myself, so embroiled in conversation that we lost track of time. For a few moments we beat Time, the insidious enemy of teaching. We never have enough. So, my students and I took it anyway. I wished I remembered what we had been discussing.

Since then, my classroom has been with teachers. I have enjoyed making this shift, despite having been warned teachers are more difficult. "They tend to chat among themselves," my new colleagues told me. At first, I saw some of this but since calling it to their attention, it has ameliorated.

But, calling attention to behaviors has a short shelf life. The real operative in my teaching focuses on quality. No amount of interactive, innovative pedagogies can make a difference without quality. But to define quality can be illusive . . .

So begins another statement of philosophy, but it will have to wait until I finish this book. These efforts, however, have served to guide me to becoming the teacher—and the writer—I want to be. Writing this book has taken this process beyond what I ever imagined.

REFLECTION

When Dan Hilliard wrote his first philosophy of education, he wondered if it would have any meaning to his teaching. He discovered that, indeed, he valued the philosophers he alluded to, especially John Dewey. Dan had a deep progressive streak, and Dewey's thinking encouraged him to make his ideas practical.

When his colleague, Pat Blackman, had to write a philosophy of his teaching for his masters degree, he asked Dan if he'd write one as well. At first he hesitated, but when he started writing, he discovered he'd shifted considerably from his first effort. When Pat and he shared, they discovered more similarities than differences, which was surprising because they often disagreed with one another at faculty meetings. Since then, they feel they understand each other better—and, more importantly, know themselves better.

Dan was now convinced that stating his philosophy was essential for his teaching. Having a philosophy statement, he said to himself, means that I know where I stand, what I believe in, and ultimately why I practice what I practice.

Pat and he then decided to establish a bi-monthly conversation group to reflect on and discuss the deeper principles and values of their work with students—and with each other. They hoped colleagues would contribute their philosophies to stimulate discussion and bring a better understanding to their teaching.

POINTS TO PURSUE

☑ Do you still have your first philosophy of education paper? If so, reread it and make a foray into a new one: one or two pages maximum.

☑ As suggested earlier in this chapter, write your philosophy with colleagues and follow the procedures offered. If you find it difficult to begin, make use of the suggested lead-ins.

☑ Do you have a different approach for periodically reexamining your teaching, such as a diary, a blog, or sending emails to teachers in other schools? If you have a different approach, share it with colleagues and invite them to participate.

☑ Writing is never easy. We should not be embarrassed to explore our thoughts in writing, especially since we want our students to write well and appropriately to their age. By looking closely at ourselves in our practice, we make it easier to ask the same from our students. Just as our reading makes us better able to entice students to read meaningfully, our writing enables us to better guide students when they write.

CHAPTER 24

Ride the Red Carpet

As with my letter to Marie (Chapter 18, "Take the Long View"), this letter is an example of the opportunities I have had as a consultant teaching new teachers. This one addresses trust—trust in ourselves and in the possibilities before us.

May 2008

Dear Molly,

I was struck by your concerns about burning out in this your first year. You work so hard! You design lessons using good content to intrigue your eighth graders. Yet, you say their lack of response, the intermittent support of your mentor (whose schedule does not blend well with yours), and the non-support of your principal frustrates you.

And, you feel alone.

Given these frustrations, I am not surprised you feel pressure to seize control. When we make this our primary goal, however, we become exhausted. We try to create perfect lessons every time, to make our rooms always appealing and neat, to return all work by the next day, to arrive early and stay late, and to work into the night and on weekends. Unless we give ourselves breaks (remember the take-care-of-me segment at our first session?), we become worn out. Your high hopes have slid into what Harry Wong calls "survival" mode and seems to be spiraling downward.[138]

I was like you in my first years, as I nearly burned out teaching history, coaching soccer and hockey, while starting a family. I often stayed up after midnight preparing lessons—and in the winter woke up at five for six o'clock hockey practices. I was lucky, however, to have good students, and support and advice from my department head and mentor. Still, I wanted to control every bit of my teaching. I wanted it to be right every day.

It was not until years later that I began to put more trust in myself. Each year before school, I spent a week (or sometimes two or three) in the classroom, to prepare for the first day, never believing I would be ready. Then, one year I realized I had always been ready and always would be. Later, when I began to apply a spiritual perspective, I put more trust in the universe, so to speak. Not everything, I began to realize, was up to me.

When I traveled with my young family to Oxfordshire, hoping to find a position in a progressive primary school in the early 1970s, I had my first taste of events falling into place, seemingly without my doing. But, that's another story. Instead, I want to share with you another time in my life where my efforts gave way to a flow, as if I had stepped onto a red carpet. While my story may seem far from your classroom, perhaps it will help you find your way to let go of the non-essentials and find a way to the grace in teaching you seek.

After nearly fifteen years teaching Russian history, Communist ideology, and George Orwell's *Animal Farm*, I developed a deep hunger to travel behind the Soviet façade to see the realities of life under communism. In the fall of 1985, I signed on to a two-week trip in October to Leningrad, Moscow, and Kiev with Bridges for Peace, a local organization then responsible for arranging ten percent of American-Soviet exchanges with Intourist, the official Soviet travel agency.

While I was thrilled to take this trip, I had reservations about traveling with a group to three of the best Soviet cities. I recalled Catherine the Great's Potemkin villages, in which she placed façades of buildings along the Volga to impress foreign visitors. Would Intourist, the official Soviet travel agency, replicate this Potemkin-village approach to convince us Americans all was well in the Soviet Union? I had little doubt. Getting closer to the façade of Soviet life would not necessarily mean I would be able to look behind it.

Still, I wanted to take this trip. At least, I would see behind the Iron Curtain perhaps to catch glimpses of the lives of average Soviets. I knew I would not be able to control the itinerary, as Intourist had planned it to the minute. If I wanted to venture on my own, it would have to be with its blessing (or I would have to slip out of the hotel or off the bus). In the end, I stayed open to what could happen rather than to try to devise ways to control events.

The first flow of fortune came in the spring when my school approved my two-week leave in October. In the summer, I attended a ten-day Russian language course at the Rassias Institute at Dartmouth College, and learned the cost was half what I expected—and my school paid part of it. During the course, I reconnected with Lilla Bradley, a parent whose children had been students of mine twenty years before.

She offered to hold a fundraiser for my trip in her home, which raised exactly the amount of money I needed (even though I had saved enough).

The trip itself continued on the red carpet the moment after I passed through customs. A perky young mother flailing wild curls with two children by her side approached me to ask if an Englishman was on our plane. I responded in my newfound but garbled Russian, culminating in "Nyet." We exchanged glances as I waited for our host. Just as our group was about to leave, I grabbed a couple of letters from my students and handed them to her children. After quickly exhausting all the Russian I knew, we resorted to pantomime and gestures. When we parted, I had a scrap of paper with her name and telephone number, and Natasha and her children, Yuri and Veronica, had two letters from America. Two days later I telephoned her from my hotel, wound my way via the metro to her apartment (virtually unheard of in those days), and began a long-time friendship with her, her husband Slava, and the children.

But on the afternoon of our first day, Molly, the most bizarre incident happened. I slipped away from the hotel carrying my camera bag over my shoulder to wander onto Nevsky Prospect, the Broadway of Leningrad. I wanted to find two Dartmouth students who were studying at Leningrad State University. I had stuffed animals from their friends in my pocket. I had no clue as to where the university was located, let alone an address—and I could not read Russian signs! While gawking at the hustle and bustle of Leningrad life, two black marketers, Alexei and his sidekick Roman, approached me, hoping to change rubles for dollars.

I resisted making an exchange and told them of my mission, "Hey, Frankie from Hollywood," said Alexei, "we are meeting these girls tonight for dinner!" "Yeah, right," I said to myself. "Of the more than six million people in this city, these two happen to know these girls!" For some reason (I really had no other option!) I decided to buy their story, for the time being anyway, as they seemed pleasant enough. At least I had someone to guide me for the afternoon—and they had a car. Before we departed, I said I had to go to the bathroom. Alexei exhorted Roman, "Take Frankie to his first real Soviet toilet," which was beneath the street—a stink I'll never forget!

Early in the evening we slipped in the back door of a restaurant where the two girls were waiting! The gathering felt so natural that I did not wonder why these girls knew Alexei and Roman. Nor did anyone at the hotel seem miffed that I had gone off on my own. Such "off-the-bus" encounters on that trip happened more often than not.

Returning home to Hanover, I became an instant celebrity and enjoyed my fifteen minutes of fame sharing absorbing stories from behind the Iron Curtain—and I had plenty! This trip proved providential, as it opened the way to seven more trips, three of them as a teacher of English to Soviet children, the first two in Leningrad with AFS Intercultural Programs and the third in Kazakhstan on my own. And would you believe, the first teacher exchange with AFS happened after I won a sabbatical leave (after years of trying!), and because my application arrived over the transom and dropped on top of the pile of applications on the day another candidate dropped out!

When I look back at this time in my life, Molly, I sometimes wonder if all of it really happened!

Since then, I believe in staying open to forces beyond my control. I admit, perhaps, it took this sequence of my Soviet trips to fully realize it. Still, "trusting the universe" has been a part of me since—most of the time.

I do not want to give you the impression these events happened out of the blue. Had I not put in years of teaching about the Russians and Soviets, practically making it my life, the red carpet to the Soviet Union would never have appeared. Without the interest, without the intent, without the desire, without the everyday teaching—and without persistence—I doubt I would have made the first trip. Had I simply trusted texts on Soviet life, I might never have considered the idea of seeing "real Russians" for myself.

Now that I think about it, I have my eighth graders to thank for making all this possible. Had I insisted they "learn from me," I might never have become open to their queries and pondered their insights as we unraveled the threads of Russian and Soviet history, particularly Orwell's *Animal Farm*. Had I concentrated on delivering from the front of the room, I may never have found doubts in my own mind about Soviet propaganda. Molly, your classroom will thrive when you and your students learn from one another. What a joy that is!

I think I was lucky to have the chance to explore the same content year after year, especially *Animal Farm*, Russian history, and Chinese philosophy. Once I knew the content from the inside, I became freer to teach from the middle of the room and let it come alive for my students. I allowed them to find their own truths rather than adopting mine in order to pass a test. Ultimately—and this has given me pause—I may have been teaching what I needed to learn.

Ironically, when I freed myself from feeling that I had to control outcomes, I may have inadvertently created red carpets for my students. Instead of thinking how I wanted them to think and reporting back to me, they became free to explore and follow their own paths. Another irony, although I have no data to support it, is that they learned more, certainly more deeply, than if they had put energy into repeating my delivery. Had I been expected to meet the demands of high-stakes tests, however, I wonder if I would have had the courage to pursue this path. I like to think I would have.

I hope that you believe your hard work and struggle will lead you towards becoming a great teacher. Your effort, care, empathy, and competence all point in the right direction. I've shared my red-carpet story as an invitation to you to trust in the process of becoming the teacher you want to become. I encourage you to step away from your belief that you need to control all aspects of your teaching. Instead, take the long view and realize your students will arrive on their last day having accomplished worthwhile learning. Know, too, your students will teach you if you allow them; they will let you know what's not working; they will show you a different path; and of course, you will have those days in which you will not connect at all.

Pay attention to what interests and excites you. As you do, you will find a red carpet at your feet to take you to unimagined places and adventures. I can see you are laying the groundwork, Molly, for a wonderful teaching life. You are taking a road you already cherish despite your struggles and pain. You are never alone as a teacher, as you've recently found a colleague next door who shares your excitement and commitment. You have all the help and support you need right in front of you, and when you seek more you will find it as well. And you have mine. Stay in touch.

Be well, be happy,
Frank

REFLECTION

When people ask Dan Hilliard if he becomes bored with teaching the same grade and the same subject, he tells them how much he loves it. "How many people," he says, "have a chance to explore what they love with students who are learning something for the first time?" He then explains how much he learns from them. Once he's prepared and taught lessons and units the first time, he has more time to assess what students are learning and to explore other ways to teach the same material. Instead of becoming easier to teach the same unit, he is able to go deeper and teach it better.

Dan is beginning to sense where he wants his teaching to take him. He figures if he pursues what he loves and does it one hundred ten percent every day, he will know his next steps. Meanwhile, he trusts that what he is doing will lead to new adventures.

POINTS TO PURSUE

☑ Sometimes when teaching becomes challenging, we often look first to external factors that interfere with our intentions. Instead, we would be wise to begin by examining our own behaviors and actions to see what we might do differently to meet challenges. Once we do this, we can gain a better perspective on other factors.

☑ If we take time to reflect on the direction of our teaching, we might find a pattern. Once we see it, we may be better able to sense our future and take steps towards fulfilling our intentions. We may also be able to ride with unexpected events and trust they will take us where we want (or need) to go.

☑ After we spend a few years creating familiar ground, we discover that we can let go of what we think we need to teach, and become more open to exploring content, skills, and values with our students. We can even let them teach us!

☑ When we feel alone, we must take steps to connect with colleagues. We cannot wait for them to come to us. Isolation serves none of us well. Don't be afraid to ask for help. Don't be afraid to let others know you need them. Teachers are very nice people.

CHAPTER 25

Create Stakeholders

As I was drafting this chapter, I heard these poignant words from Sir Ken Robinson, Ted Talk contributor: "The first boy said, 'I bring you gold.' And the second boy said, 'I bring you myrrh.' And the third boy said, 'Frank sent this.'"[139] In one sentence he reveals the fundamental flaw in teaching in today's pressurized, over-extended, and misdirected classrooms. Teaching to the test has meant flying through facts without regard to meaning. Children are forced to absorb fragmented knowledge, preventing them from finding significance in the world, let alone in themselves.

It's no wonder they do not choose to do their schoolwork. The ubiquitous presence of text messaging, video games, iPods, cell phones, television, and the Internet hold far greater appeal. On-screen interactions, often at home alone, prevail over face time with their peers and lure them away from homework.

Sometimes I imagine them as pebbles skipping over water. They move quickly but not deeply. They make innumerable contacts but do not linger. They connect but do not embrace. They travel fast but do not saunter—and do not know how.

Yet, they come to us in kindergarten as mobile kids with exploring thumbs and minds, natives to the electronic devices they touch with glee. They step through the classroom door eager to explore, but we say, "No, not yet." Soon, they learn to curb their curiosity. By third grade, they are less curious, less interested, less connected. We continue, however, to postpone exploration in the name of coverage, of impending state and federal assessments, of preparing for next year.

We feel caught in a conundrum. We now teach very different children who process the world in ways unknown to us. We see them often as impatient and inattentive. They appear more urbane, yet less mature.

Parents also seem baffled, as they try to sort out their confusions about growing up in today's culture. Parents—and teachers—often speak about children as, "bright," implying with confidence they'll be heading off to an Ivy League school. Or, they'll say, "Wow, what an athlete already! Look at him dribble the ball!" As natural as this praise may be, we need to remember that we cannot know the future of any child any more than we knew of our own future. How can we, then, move away from our quick-judgment tendencies, particularly when we do it mainly for our convenience?

At a summer faculty workshop, Drew Gibson, formerly a history teacher at Berkshire Arts and Technology Public Charter School and now at Mt. Greylock Regional High School in Massachusetts, raised the issue of making students shareholders in the classroom. His argument focused on the importance of teachers encouraging students to take "ownership" in their learning, instead of acting as "cognitive slaves," who only do the minimum to reach their goals. Citing his understanding of the slave South, Gibson related unmotivated students to slaves, who had acted passively in part because they had no stake in the work they were forced to do.

As the discussion progressed, we agreed that those students who only do the minimum care less about their future. We also agreed that we have a responsibility to motivate and create ways to invoke effort into their work. Those who become stakeholders take ownership in whatever they do, and therefore focus their attention on everything. Teachers who are stakeholders also take ownership in what they teach. They, too, own and not simply deliver. They teach from the middle of the room.

Writer Steve Almond, in a perceptive column in the *Boston Globe*, raised the issue of the shallowness of many blogs, in which literary bloggers bear "more resemblance to talk show hosts than a literary salon." He fears that the ease with which bloggers write tempts them to be more quick than deep. He cites newspapers trying to win over digital readers with blogs for fear of losing their readership altogether. He's concerned, however, that newspapers may, in fact, be ". . . quickening their own demise. What young readers lack isn't a tolerance for newsprint, but the will to investigate [to take ownership in] the troubled world that exists outside their various flashing screens."[140] However, the jury on blogging is still out, because it will surely morph into new—and, hopefully, more sophisticated—forms.

There are similar concerns about the influence of Google. One teacher I know feels that Google may be replacing his students' memories. "Why remember information," his students argue, "when all we need to do is Google whatever we need to know?" I wonder if such an attitude, as Nicholas Carr in *The Atlantic* intimates, will result in Google becoming our collective human brain?[141] I hint at this point in workshops when I ask, "What is the capital of Iowa?" I pause and then say, "Google!" My point is that we don't need to memorize states and capitals, because we can find them instantly. We don't need such information in our heads, because we know where to find it. But, I stress that we must know how to determine the validity of information, and discuss it intelligently.

Still, the larger question remains, "What do we need to learn, to memorize in the twenty-first century?" The times tables? Regions of the world? Literary terms? The causes of the Civil War? Living in a culture in which Google surrounds us in ever-expanding ways, we need to address what *do* we need to know. Given that we are preparing students for jobs that don't exist yet; given that we do not know the problems we will be facing in ten years; and given that we do not know the technologies and knowledge we'll acquire in that time, it behooves us to wrestle with these fundamental questions:

> What do students need to know, understand, and be able to do?
> What competencies must they have to face the unknown future?
> What values should we nurture for them, for our communities, and for the global world?
> How can students (and teachers) become stakeholders in their lives and in the lives of others?

We must not be afraid to tackle these questions and confront those who are unwilling to face them. We must be willing to challenge people who demand that our students take assessments that only test for knowledge and skills that were useful in the past. We must advocate for our students and their future, and insist we give them the best we can. Anything less and we will cheat them.

It's becoming obvious, even to casual observers, that the more time people spend using electronic devices, the less time they dwell inside their own minds. How much time would a person who averages thirty-five thousand text messages per month (outside her job) have for reflection?[142] Will the relentless attraction of social media lure us to become conduits of information rather than creators of thoughts? Such questions generate other questions for teachers:

> How can we invite students to explore and value their own minds, their own thoughts, and step away from temptations to slide in and out of electronic media?
>
> How can we slow students' learning while respecting their newfound faculties?
>
> How can we take the tools of social media and use them to foster reflective, meaningful, and resourceful thinking to serve students' growth and the greater good of others?
>
> What are our moral obligations to respond to this new way of learning?
>
> How are humans becoming different as they learn more from screens and less from each other?
>
> Do we want to hold back the tide, because we do not know how to ride it as our children do? What can we do? What should we do?

We need to teach children how to own their work. If we continue to insist on lectures, worksheets, fact-based tests, and formulaic papers, we treat them as cognitive slaves. We foster obedience rather than thinking. Instead, we must nurture their dreams, ideals, creativity, and passions, and we must be honest and listen until they know we are indeed listening. We need to show students how knowing and understanding are fundamental to being human.

How do we do this? In a later communication, Gibson recalled an old adage, "You can lead a horse to water, but you can't make him drink," which he modified to, "You can lead a child to knowledge, but you can't make him *think*." He continued the analogy, likening the offer of salt to the horse to spur drinking to teachers offering multiple open doorways to cause students to learn. This is one of the central themes of this book.

Therefore, we cannot abrogate our responsibility to share the eternal human values we have developed over the past ten thousand years. If we give up the human treasure of face-to-face contact by allowing technological wizardry to supplant it, we will, ironically, become separated from one another. Students who walk home from school with classmates while on cell phones or texting are already living alone. When they arrive at home, they lock the door and are left with media devices as their means of befriending each other. Friends without breath, without touch, without a wet glint in their eyes.

We need to find ways to incorporate the changing world of technology into our teaching, but on a deeper level than how students use them. We need to slow the skipping stones and encourage them to probe where they land. At the same time that we acknowledge that the capital of Iowa is Google, we also need to demonstrate the importance of learning the arguments presented in the Federalist Papers, analyze Orwell's metaphors in *Animal Farm*, interpret the implications of Catherine the Great's Potemkin Villages, consider the impact of sunspots on climate change, and learn processes to aid thinking, such as the times tables.

And, we need to teach the joys of ambiguity and wondering.

REFLECTION

Dan Hilliard has seen how his students have bought into the glitz of electronic devices. A few students even attempt to text during his classes. He has been hesitant, however, to shut down or take away cell phones, as he does not want to be known as a dinosaur. After all, he has an iPhone—and has used it occasionally in class to call a friend for an opinion during a class discussion or to Google to clarify a fact. He once even asked his students to take out their cell phones to contact friends for their opinion on a controversial issue before the class. They loved it—and it activated the discussion. He plans to do more with cell phones in class.

When he learned about TeacherTube videos, "Did You Know? 2.0" and later "Did You Know? 3.0," (A.K.A. Shift Happens)[143] he decided to ask his principal if he could show "3.0" at a faculty meeting. He felt that everyone should be in touch with the information presented in these videos, not only for their content but also to open the faculty to using resources including YouTube, TeacherTube, iTunes U, TED.com, and Bigthink.com. His own distaste for textbooks has led him to these sources as a means for keeping his materials up-to-date and appealing to students.

Dan is convinced that if every teacher watched one Ted Talk each week, they would change their teaching—or would certainly enhance it. He suggested beginning with, "Ken Robinson Says Schools Kill Creativity."[144]

POINTS TO PURSUE

☑ Do you see today's children "as pebbles skipping over water?" Are you able to convince them to dig deep into what you teach? Do they resist? Do you understand how your students learn best?

☑ "Why is it the longer kids are in school, the less curious they seem?" A private school administrator asked this question in Tony Wagner's, *The Global Achievement Gap*.[145] What do we do to contribute to decreasing curiosity in school? What can we do to recapture it, nurture it, and celebrate it? What are the consequences when we don't?

☑ In response to parental (and teacher) tendencies to judge and project children's skills, how can we make room for children to discover themselves? How can we prevent prejudgments from interfering with our children's growth?

☑ How has Google evolved in your teaching? In your life? Have you absorbed the radical impact Google is having on all of us? Do you know what your children need to know, understand, and be able to do—beyond Google?

☑ Recognizing we are "digital immigrants" and not "digital natives" (as Marc Prensky writes[146]), or "refugees" and not "mobile kids" (as Neil Swidey writes[147]), how can we reconcile students' fluency and ease with these technologies with what we believe we need to teach? This may be the fundamental question of our time as teachers.

CHAPTER 26

Begin at the End

On the first day of school, we feel the pull of the last day whether we attend to it or not.[148] We begin in September and end in June. We compose our lives inside beginnings and endings. Most of them work out somewhat as expected, but others surprise us.

Most of us "have kids" for a year. In that time span, there are scheduled vacations and holidays; semesters, terms, and marking periods; lessons, units of study, and courses; musicals, concerts, and plays; and sports seasons. We welcome the New Year as a chance to begin anew; new teachers especially find solace in this second chance, as do their students. We live inside blocks of time and set our lives to their rhythms.

We think in weeks, as well. Many of us use Thursdays as review days for Friday tests. Mondays and Fridays, too, have their own feel, their own energy. When we are tired or discouraged, Fridays come slowly and Mondays come too quickly. When we are excited and in a groove, we look forward to Mondays and milk as much as we can from the last hour on Friday.

The first day of school is special: a clean slate, a fresh start, a new beginning, and a level playing field (for that day at least). Nothing like it really!

Given all these beginnings and endings, we are often challenged to keep pace as glitches and surprises upset our rhythm. New teachers wonder why no one prepared them for these hits. It didn't seem as confusing when they were in school. Student teaching, they quickly discover, only touches the surface of real school, since its impossible to replicate being alone in classrooms.

So, how can we prepare to meet the perplexities of daily school life? How can we set our priorities and not lose sight of what matters, of what we want students to know and care about? We observe fellow teachers who seem able to weather storms well, who keep their composure no matter the amount of stress. We quickly learn that there are no magic bullets to help us manage the chaos, no formulas to make our classrooms calm and productive. We need to find our own means, our own anchors to stabilize our ship.

We drop anchor when we choose to build our teaching towards known outcomes. We can define the roads we intend to take, knowing we may discover new and better roads along the way. In the words of Robert Frost, we might even claim at some later date that we "took the one less traveled by" and believe it "has made all the difference."[149] But, we won't know until we commit to it. Many roads lead to Rome; we need to choose ours.

"Footprints. It is all about footprints." So began a letter to my students and their parents in my last year in the classroom. I had often designed roadmaps for the year ahead, particularly for my open-education classroom, but I had never articulated it in a letter on the first day of class. I was intrigued with the effect of this piece, not only on the intended audience and me, but also on others since then. I have no doubt that this response led me to develop a portfolio assignment for a course I teach on backward design, which invited teachers to imagine standing at the door of their classroom on the last day of school. I begin explaining this assignment by describing the following scenario:

> It's the last day of school. You are standing outside your door. Your children are leaving. You know they will no longer be yours.
>
> You ask yourself: Who are they now? What have they become? What have they learned? How will they think? How will they relate to the world? To each other? What do they understand about themselves? What is important to them? What do they care about? What do they value? What differences have I made?
>
> Take some time to reflect on these questions. Most likely you will begin considering personal, emotional, and intellectual qualities; hardly anyone mentions success with grades.

After a pause, I continue:

> We need to know as teachers what we want for our students. We chose to teach because we believe we can make a difference. Regardless of the demands for testing and accountability, we understand in our heart of hearts the deeper obligations and responsibilities we have to them.
>
> We need to articulate what our students have to learn, understand, and be able to do—every class, every day through out the year. We need to provide the means for students to assess what they learn as often as

we can. And, we need to design instruction that reaches out to all learners. We do not always practice these principles, but we try.

Writing an end-of-the-year reflection, then, provides us with a benchmark for planning lessons and units of study. Our own words remind us to put lessons and units in context of the whole, so the overarching understandings, knowledge and skills, and essential questions to drive our students' thinking stay aligned. They benefit because they have the opportunities to connect and make sense of what we ask them to learn.

A teacher who gives students the final exam on the first day of school understands this.

Then I take time to refer to the importance of backwards design planning, which is based on the work of Grant Wiggins and Jay McTighe.[150] Usually some of my students already know about this approach, and many recognize that they instinctively use backwards-design principles. After briefly describing it, I then explain its potential impact:

Backwards design has become an essential tool for classroom teachers. Its principles and practices are comprehensive and accessible, albeit sometimes complex. It hits a "sweet spot" in our teaching. When using it, we not only see the whole but also how the parts fit together. We sense alignment and coherence in our teaching from day to day. We see ourselves moving in harmony alongside our students.

Something else happens, too. Backwards design thinking invokes the spirit. When we become immersed, we not only become engaged, but emotionally committed as well; I have observed (and experienced) this response often.

Unlike developing traditional curriculum units, backwards design requires engagement. As we become involved, we seek collaboration with colleagues. As the process deepens, we invite students into the process; we tell them where we are headed, how they will be assessed, and what they will have to do. Once we see backward design's clarity of purpose and direction, we develop a visceral response to what we teach and pass it on to our students and colleagues. Our classrooms literally come alive.

I conclude by explaining the end-of-the-year assignment, rephrasing my first scenario:

> Begin your reflection, then, by envisioning your students leaving your classroom on their last day. What do you want them to take with them? What kind of people should they be? What do you want them to think? To care about? To imagine?
>
> Whatever your big questions, can you visualize the end-in-view you are aiming for? Can you see the big picture you want for your students? Can you articulate the overall purpose of your teaching in this context—the purpose all your units and lessons will point toward? What is your ultimate backwards design?
>
> Trust that after completing this reflection, you will have a clear sense of your purpose and will be better able to design coherent learning for your students. Successful change, after all, begins at the end. We are in the business of change. Students change before our eyes. Our lessons change, too, once in contact with our students. We need to design learning to direct these changes towards worthwhile and productive goals. Having a vision of the whole is essential.
>
> Write well. I look forward to reading what you have to say.

Before we conclude our discussion, I then repeat: "A teacher who gives students the final exam on the first day of school understands this." We then examine Dan Bisaccio's "Biology Final" that he gives to his biology students on the first day of classes (Figure 26.1).[151] While I do not expect most will follow Bisaccio's lead, we usually have provocative discussions. When we finish, everyone agrees that Bisaccio has a clear vision of what he wants his students to know, understand, and be able to do; there is no doubt that he will have a good idea of what his students have accomplished by the time they walk out the door on the last day of school—and they will as well.

Most of us would hesitate to pass out our final exams on the first day of school, as it defies the traditional role of exams. Our teachers and professors used them to determine our grades, and perhaps, (at least they may have thought) our intelligence. We took exams seriously and we tried to guess what they would ask. I never played the game well.

More often than not, you will find the definition of "biology" given in a somewhat clinical manner such as, "Biology is the study of life and how organisms relate to their physical environs." However, biologists are in the business of seeking answers to questions, and their search encompasses a much more exciting and broader spectrum than this usual definition implies.

This year you will be the biologist and, in seeking the answers to the questions posed below (and others that will certainly arise), you will have the opportunity to discover and understand a much more comprehensive definition of biology than the one previously stated.

From time to time you will be given the following questions to answer . . . and, in fact, this is your final exam as well. Each time you answer them, your grade will be based on your development as a biologist. In other words, as the year unfolds, it is expected that you will become more and more the "sophisticated biologist," and your answers should reflect this.

1. Define "biology" in your own words.

2. What characterizes life? In other words: What is the difference between "living" and "non-living," and between "living" and "never-living?"

3. There are 5 Kingdoms of Life: What are they? What is common to all? What distinguishes each as a separate kingdom?

4. From a scientific standpoint: How did life begin on this planet? What characteristics of this planet enabled life to evolve? What were some problems early organisms needed to overcome and how did they do it?

5. Within the 5 Kingdoms, biologists recognize millions of species. What is a "species?" Why are there so many different species? In terms of Question 4, how did so many forms of life come to be?

6. Perhaps the most essential biochemical reactions are listed below. In terms of entropy (2nd Law of Thermodynamics), discuss the importance of these reactions as they pertain to life:

$$6CO_2 + 6 H_2O + SUNLIGHT \rightarrow C_6H_{12}O_6 + 6O_2$$
$$C_6H_{12}O_6 + 6O_2 \rightarrow 6CO_2 + 6H_2O + ENERGY$$

7. In an ecological sense, interpret the essay "Thinking Like a Mountain," written by Aldo Leopold, from his book, *A Sand County Almanac.*

Figure 26.1.

Biology Final.

(From Dan Bisaccio's "Biology Final," in Robert Fried, *The Passionate Teacher*, 1995.)

What if we decided to follow Dan Bisaccio's example and give our final exam at the beginning of the year? Would we be lowering our standards? Would we be making it easier for our students? Would we "teach to the test" more, rather than teach for learning?

However, if we take time to reflect on his intentions, we would realize that his Biology Final becomes a vehicle for his students to become biologists, not for getting As on the exam. When his students define biology in their own words in September, they most likely will write a paragraph or two, but by May they'll compose a thoughtful essay. Bisaccio assesses their growth as biologists, not for what they remember or recall. Students improve in class as biologists, as athletes improve at practices for games. He teaches by visualizing students leaving his lab on the last day as biologists.

Finally, the essay "Big Rocks" reminds us to set priorities. Given the increasing complexities of teaching, this essay gives us pause to consider our values and to make those we cherish our top priorities.

One day an expert was speaking to a group of business students, and to drive home a point, he used an illustration those students will never forget.

As this man stood in front of the group of high-powered overachievers, he said, "Okay, time for a quiz." He pulled out a one-gallon, wide-mouthed mason jar and set it on a table in front of him. Then he produced about a dozen fist-sized rocks and carefully placed them, one at a time, into the jar. When the jar was filled to the top and no more rocks would fit inside, he asked, "Is this jar full?"

Everyone in the class said, "Yes."

Then he said, "Really?" He reached under the table and pulled out a bucket of gravel. Then he dumped some gravel in and shook the jar causing pieces of gravel to work themselves down into the spaces between the big rocks. Then he asked the group once more, "Is the jar full?"

By this time, the class was onto him. "Probably not," one of them answered.

"Good!" he replied. He reached under the table and brought out a bucket of sand. He started dumping the sand in and it went into all the spaces left between the rocks and the gravel. Once more, he asked the question, "Is this jar full?"

"No!" the class shouted.

Once again, he said, "Good!" Then he grabbed a pitcher of water and began to pour it in until the jar was filled to the brim. Then he looked up at the class and asked, "What is the point of this illustration?"

One eager beaver raised his hand and said, "The point is, no matter how full your schedule is, if you try really hard, you can always fit some more things into it!"

"No," the speaker replied, "that's not the point. The truth this illustration teaches us is: If you don't put the big rocks in first, you'll never get them in at all."

What are the big rocks in your life? A project you want to accomplish? Time with your loved ones? Your faith? Your education? Your finances? A cause? Teaching or mentoring others? Remember to put these big rocks in first or you'll never get them in at all.

So, when you are reflecting on this story, ask yourself this question: "What are the big rocks in my life or in my teaching?" Then, put those in your jar first.[152]

As the Mad Hatter said, "If you don't know where you are going, any road will take you there." Given the short time we have with students, we need to know the road we'll take together. We need to establish it in every course, unit, and lesson. Whether or not we choose a less traveled road, we can have the confidence that we will make a difference.

REFLECTION

When Dan Hilliard saw Dan Bisaccio's Biology Final in Rob Fried's *The Passionate Teacher*, he had an epiphany. "What a difference," he said to himself, "A final exam as an indicator of the quality and depth of thinking, rather than as a scorecard of what his students remembered (or not)! If I could use this idea in my classroom, I could merge the process of my teaching with my intended outcomes. I could invite my students into the circle of my intentions, and we could explore together the ever-growing and changing knowledge, understandings, and skills inherent in twenty-first century learning."

He couldn't wait to tell his colleagues, so he sent an email to everyone with Dan Bisaccio's Biology Final attached. He knew that his message would raise many questions. He wondered, too, about the applicability of Bisaccio's final-exam concept for those teachers who did not give exams. He suspected, however, that it would at least stir thinking and perhaps help clarify everyone's direction and purpose.

POINTS TO PURSUE

- ☑ Have you ever "dropped anchor" by writing an end-of-the-year reflection? Take some time, even if in the middle of the year, to imagine standing at your classroom door on the last day of school. Imagine your students passing by, taking "you" with them. What do they leave with? What difference have you made? This is well worth your time.

- ☑ What is the rhythm of your classroom? Does most of what you do happen because you've always done it? Or, do you consciously create rhythms to spur curiosity and inquisitiveness? Or, are your rhythms based primarily on your needs? Take a "rhythm inventory" of your year to find out.

- ☑ How do you react to Dan Bisaccio's giving his final on the first day of school? How might any of us—at any grade level, in any position— implement his thinking to deepen our teaching? Explore his idea with colleagues to elicit their reactions. Who knows where the conversation might lead?

- ☑ Share "Big Rocks" with colleagues. Better yet, share it with your students and provide time for thoughtful consideration. Given that their lives are filled with distractions, finding their big rocks might help them sort out their priorities. It is such a simple, yet profound, story.

CHAPTER 27

Make a Difference

When we teach, we make a difference. We decide to teach because we want to make a difference, as teachers have before us. Veterans tell stories of students who write or call to thank them. But, we demur from taking credit, because we are modest. Taking credit, perhaps, opens us for taking blame as well.

Nonetheless, we need to know that we make a difference every day, and at the same time, not orchestrate the differences we make. We need to act on behalf of our students at all times. We need to encourage them at every opportunity and discourage them only when necessary. We need to see their potential, not only their limitations. We need to offer opportunities rather than close doors. And, we need to treat them as individuals, never the same as anyone else.

Most of us do not hear often from our former students, particularly when we teach in grades below high school. When we do we are often surprised—and certainly honored. Warm comments from parents and the occasional letter from a student remind us of the differences we made.

One instance in my later years stands out, not only because it warmed my heart, but also because it taught me that we are not in charge of outcomes as hard as we might try. I wrote this story in response to an appeal from National Public Radio (NPR) for Christmas stories several years ago.

The real gift came many years later.

It began with my wish to give a winter coat to a newspaper girl. It was late November 1992 when the cold hit hard in Worcester. Each Sunday on the way to church, we would pass through the intersection of Park and Highland Streets, where she helped her father sell the *Telegram & Gazette*. A small, dark-haired girl, about ten, she was with him every Sunday. Occasionally, I would buy a paper.

As the weather intensified, I noticed she only had a thin fall jacket. When the first blizzard came, she still wore the same jacket. I decided, then, to find her a warmer coat. I did not have the money to buy a new one, so I invited my eighth graders to help me. While I am not clear as to why I asked them, it must have been the right idea. One of my students, Katie, arrived the next day with a lilac down parka—in the perfect size.

I placed the coat into a colorful bag with an unsigned card. As I drove to church, I became nervous and concerned as to whether I was doing the right thing. At school, we had asked students to bring gifts to be distributed by Social Services. My students and I bought gifts at a local mall and wrapped them for a little boy. Now, I was having second thoughts about giving the girl the coat myself. I prayed for the light to turn red at the intersection. It did. I jumped out of the car, ran up to her, handed her the bag, said "Merry Christmas" to her and her father, and jumped back into the car. When I told the story an hour later, I could not hold back tears.

Giving her the coat had been an obsession. That she chose not to wear it most of the rest of the winter Sundays, however, became a mystery. I struggled to accept that my gift of the coat, as all gifts, needed to be unconditional.

Eight years later and a couple of weeks before Christmas, I held my final class with a group of new teachers I had been working with since September. As part of our closing, I had given them stationery and envelopes on which to write a thank-you letter to someone who made a difference to their becoming a teacher, someone whom they had not yet thanked.

When I returned home that evening, I found such a letter from Katie, the student who had given me the coat. Needless to say, I was deeply touched not only because she had taken the time to write but also by her gratitude. After expressing thanks for helping her survive eighth grade, she wrote, "At one point when you were my advisor, you encouraged me to donate a coat to a young girl you saw out in the cold each Sunday, selling newspapers. I cannot even begin to tell you how much this changed my life. Years later when I was deciding what to become in my life, I thought back to that time and realized my calling to become a nurse."

The real gift was one I never imagined.

I had been obsessed with giving a coat to a freezing newspaper girl who rarely wore it. Instead, the real gift belonged to Katie, whose action, unbeknownst to her at the time, changed her life. As the Bhagavad Gita says, we should not become attached to the results of our actions. Such understanding frees us to do what we need to do and move on. It reminds us that teaching is not about us, but about our students.

In essence, we simply don't know when and how we make a difference. We can, however, make it our intention to seek learning instead of talking, insisting that students copy notes, and hissing at them to be quiet. When we intend to see them learning, we concentrate on connecting, and if we're lucky, we see their light and let it shine. We can be confident that we create possibilities for joy—hopefully theirs and certainly ours.

A second story, which I wrote for "A Celebration of Teachers," in Lebanon, New Hampshire in May 2006, revealed its true meaning only when I delivered it. I intended to focus on teaching from the middle of the room, but as I was speaking, I realized it was about trusting and letting go of having all students fulfill the same expectation at the same time.

> Teaching invites internal conflicts. We tell students, for example, what we expect for a project, give them a specific due date, and work alongside them along the way. Yet, on the day the projects are due, one or more students fail to pass it in. What then?
>
> As you may remember from George Orwell's *Animal Farm*, Napoleon, the Stalin pig, seizes power from Snowball, the more gentle and idealistic pig. My students and I used to argue about why dictatorship was permitted to triumph over idealism. I contended that Snowball caused his own demise and Napoleon needed to remove him. Our heated discussions carried over to the dinner table.
>
> For his final project, Jeff wanted to create a series of cartoons to explore his understanding of *Animal Farm*. The book had affected him deeply, and he wanted to share his feelings and ideas.
>
> A day or two before the projects were due, his cartoon idea folded, as he simply could not finish it. I felt badly for him, as I knew he wanted to make it work. When the projects arrived, his was not among them. I pondered what to do with Jeff. I knew we were expected to hold all students accountable. But, I decided not to confront him, but to wait and see.

Sometime later, Jeff passed in his project, which he entitled "The Fellowship of the Farm," a rewrite of the last part of the book.

Instead of capitulating to Napoleon, Jeff wrote, Snowball suddenly returns, rallies a few of the other animals and—reminiscent of Gandhi's courage in speaking truth to power—walks up the path to Napoleon's quarters, taking the physical abuse of the guards but not stopping. Napoleon emerges and they talk, and through the miracle of Jeff's writing, Napoleon concedes to the new commandments for fellowship.

I have never forgotten Jeff's belief in the power of peace. In "The Fellowship of the Farm," he shared his worldview. As we read his fable, we knew we were in the presence of someone special.

Sometime early in my teaching, I understood the need to step off the stage and into the middle of the room. I needed to talk less and to open my eyes and ears—and my intuition. I needed to let go of the protective shell of teaching, as I was taught to teach, and instead to open up to learning alongside my students. Had I continued to teach from the front of the room and insisted that Jeff pass his project in with everyone else's, he might never have shown me his heart in his work.

At the time I prepared this talk, I wanted to share Jeff's revision of the Seven Commandments for his Fellowship Farm, but I could not find his paper. A year later I came across it and discovered that Jeff had alluded to Gandhi's *The Story of My Experiments with Truth*. Jeff called his commandments, "The New Seven Truths to Live By," though he only wrote six:

Each animal can improve himself to be better.
Animals must never use violence to solve difficulties.
Animals must respect each other.
Animals must be able to sacrifice themselves to resist a bad system.
All animals must work together to their ability to support themselves.
There is a force of good that supports the work of each animal.

An eighth grader invoking Gandhi. It was worth the wait. Jeff now teaches English at a university in Taiwan, and he's become a father. He tells me his students speak well of him. I am not surprised.

REFLECTION

As we seek to know ourselves, we need to acknowledge that we make a difference, and we must recognize that, more often than not, we will never know when or how. We must never underestimate the impact we have on others. But, ironically, we cannot make this our focus. If we do, we will spend time looking for the differences we make (or think we are making) rather than making those differences. We would be like the athlete who edits his play during the game and thereby loses focus. We need to teach well each day to make learning happen in our classrooms. We must join Dan Hilliard and teach from the middle of the room.

Hidden Expectations

I awoke at four o'clock in the morning and scribbled the following on a Post-it: "the time of inaction merges into action to discover the hidden expectations of the reader . . ."

A couple of days later, I found the Post-it. "What does this mean?" I asked myself. "What was I thinking?" I didn't have a clue. I could only begin to speculate. I knew, however, it had to do with writing this book.

Perhaps, I pondered, it was about identifying with my future readers. As I write, I often pause to contemplate as I search to anticipate potential readers' internal needs, wishes, and purposes. Ironically, this is about tapping into their deepest desires not yet articulated in my mind.

Writing without readers, after all, is like playing catch with myself. The poet writes alone in the attic room but his poetry arrives when someone reads it. The artist paints by herself but the paintings emerge in the viewer. So, is it not the same for the writer?

I have sat nearly every day for more than three years writing primarily to teachers. I explore ideas and peruse the imaginable, and sometimes the unimaginable. I speak to my readers as I write, but all along I am waiting for them to open the book. When they do, the book will have arrived.

I discovered this truth when parts of my lost manuscript on teaching and living in the Soviet Union, which I wrote in the late 1980s, appeared on a Kazakh blog in 2008! One September day, I Googled my name and there it was—my insights on the ubiquitous cheating in Soviet classrooms in eight installments entitled, *Encounters with Soviet People*. A young American university professor (I later discovered) had retyped sections to share with her Kazakh students, in an effort to end their continuing practice of this old Soviet behavior. Suddenly, I felt a piece of my manuscript had come alive, connecting to readers awaiting its message. (How she discovered the manuscript is another story.)

But then I wondered, perhaps my early morning rumination on the Post-it was about me. The phrase, "time of inaction merges into moments of action," speaks to the writer's process. Fingering the keyboard inside innumerable pauses, I write, so I think, to discover my readers, but perhaps I am really discovering myself. Aha! Maybe my meditation has validity from both the writer and reader's points of view.

Returning to the Soviet manuscript, I realize I did not invent the message the blogger attempted to convey to her Kazakh students. Yes, I had observed blatant cheating at all levels in Soviet schools, both for tests and in prompting one another during lessons. But my choice to write to expose this practice did not begin with me, but derived from people who taught me the value of honesty—and from my distaste with my own dishonesty.

What does it mean, then, for a writer to have the urge to discover the hidden expectations of his readers? Perhaps my call to write—and it's clearly a calling—comes from a deep desire to tap into the awaiting minds and hearts of my future readers, especially teachers. I see them waiting to make needed discoveries.

I wonder, then, as I continue to observe teachers and write, whether my invitations already exist in their minds but are, at this point, hidden and unrealized. They were hidden from me, too, when I began this book. I first wrote in the third person and pointed fingers at teachers and schools; only later did I shift to the first person and create invitations. Was this a process of self-discovery, anticipating the self-discovery of my readers? Given that the acts of giving and receiving are equivalent, so, then, might a similar equation exist between writers and readers?

Perhaps writing this book rests on my belief that I write to make visible the invisible in my readers. My job is to awaken, as I've been awakened by books, teachers, students, colleagues, friends, parents, and children—and from my own writing. Do we arrive in this life on a mission to become one with who we already are? Is that our purpose? Whenever we encounter a provocative book, a difficult child, or a challenging class, are we not given the opportunity to discover our own hidden expectations?

Perhaps we choose our life paths as teacher, doctor, restaurateur, carpenter, writer, and so on, to open our doors of self-discovery.

Maybe the metaphor with which I awoke that morning really does cut both ways. It is about me *and* about my future readers.

To extend this metaphor as a teacher, could it be true that we take the "time of inaction merging into moments of action to discover the hidden expectations" *of our students*? Could it be true that their hidden expectations are our challenge? Are not we responsible to teach to these hidden expectations—at least doing our best to anticipate them? And should we not seek to discover our own? After all, we are heading into an unknown future, more so than at any other time in human history. Knowing ourselves can anchor us as we face the unforeseen.

The time of "inaction," then, is essential, because we cannot simply carry on as we have. We must pause to consider the new and previously unimagined. We need to discover approaches to integrate the new ways of our students into what we know and value. We need to be willing to return to inaction when what we are doing is not working, or when students tell us it's not working. Plowing on, pushing through, covering material, completing the textbook on time, drilling for tests . . . these are the enemies of becoming who we are—and for students becoming who they are.

A Teaching Manifesto

In deciding to change our practice from teaching from the front of the room to the middle, we need guidelines to remind us and guide us. By signing this "Teaching Manifesto," we commit to making this happen.

For myself:

- I will use invitations in my teaching and be relentless in finding those that work.
- I will make the love and joy of learning the centerpiece of my instruction.
- I will listen more and talk less. I will ask more questions and give fewer answers. My questions will elicit thinking and not right responses.
- I will refrain from repeating what students say as respect for their voice.
- I will listen for the wonder in each child and nourish it every day. I will see the world from their point of view.
- I will respect different learning styles and seek pathways to assure successes for each student.
- I will investigate and incorporate relevant conclusions of brain research.
- I will teach by invoking high expectations for all students and recognize I may not know what they may be. Every day, I will reexamine my perceptions of each child's potential.
- I will articulate the learning intentions from the big picture of what I'm to teach into each lesson—and I will make sure each student always understands where we are headed and why.

- I will teach meaningful and worthwhile content, skills, and values, including important ideas from the past, as well as issues and concerns for the future.
- I will bring big ideas and enduring understandings into the classroom and value my students' interpretations of them.
- I will understand my fundamental responsibility to teach for lifelong learning: to teach students to teach themselves.
- I will seek what is authentic in myself and in my teaching, and commit to discovering my passions and invoke them in my classroom.
- I commit to understand the world in which I live so I can offer honest and informed perspectives.
- I will model risk-taking to teach my students the value of frustration and struggle in learning challenging material.
- I will seek to be open to innovative ideas, concepts, and pedagogies to improve my teaching.
- I will build on methods that work and jettison those that do not.
- I commit to stay current in the growing knowledge base of the profession and in my content areas, and seek collaboration to integrate best practices into my teaching.
- I will welcome colleagues, parents, and interested citizens into my classroom to share in our adventures. I know I cannot teach alone, and I cannot teach without feedback and support.
- I will understand my teaching as a calling and not as a job.
- I commit to moving into the middle of the room and encourage students to learn every day, in every class.

With my colleagues:[153]

- We will pay attention to what works and what does not.

- We will take every word, every event, every failure and turn them to the advantage of our students, sweeping nothing under the rug.

- We will recognize our part when students struggle, and together we will find ways for them to achieve success.

- We will not blame officials, parents, or students for our lack of success. If we cannot enlist their commitment, we will be relentless in doing all we can to overcome challenges and difficulties. No excuses.

- No hurdle, no matter how high, will deny us the opportunity to serve our students best interests by invoking intelligence, compassion and love.

And, in addition, I/we will...

•

•

•

Signed: _____ Date: _____

Acknowledgments

Teachers stand on the shoulders of countless others. Before I decided to become a teacher, I owed much to my teachers who allowed me to see them as they were. Miss Karasack, in fourth grade, sensed I was fidgety and made me her postman, so I could deliver and gather all her messages. Miss Mason, in sixth grade, barely taller than we were, openly expressed her emotions; I remember her tears as she read Longfellow's "Evangeline." Thomas Donovan, at Mount Hermon, despite his sarcasm and distain for some students, demonstrated the power of the intellect to engage young minds. Charlie Keller, family friend and professor, encouraged me as I was growing up to consider becoming a teacher. Orville Murphy, history professor at Williams, saw enough potential in my pursuit to understand history to nominate me for a senior seminar—a little late unfortunately because of my earlier grades. And, Sidney Eisen not only provoked my thinking—he also once granted me (so I believe) a C– that enabled me to stay in college.

Once I committed to teaching, I absorbed as much as possible from my fellow graduate students at Wesleyan's MAT program, particularly those who lived in our "Bumpaleeno State" residence on High Street. I treasured, too, Professor Reginald Archambault's philosophical musings and Ernest Stabler's gentle guidance. My student teaching in nearby Meriden titillated my desire to have my own classroom, which materialized in my first contract to teach ninth-grade European History and twelfth-grade Problems of Democracy at Hanover High School in New Hampshire. I am indebted to my first students upon whose shoulders I began pursuing my dream—and to each and every student with whom I've been blessed to have had in my classroom. Without students we do not teach; without mine, I would not have become the teacher I am.

Perhaps my deepest debt belongs to Delmar W. Goodwin, who took me under his wing as department chair that first year and asked if he could co-teach my low-tracked, street-smart seniors with me. What became an extra class for him meant a mentor for me. Del openly shared his wisdom, patience, and creativity and took time to observe me with my ninth graders. His uncanny perception of my gifts (and shortcomings) took me to the eighth grade the next year, where I could become more innovative and creative in teaching Area Studies—and he encouraged me to teach Senior Electives as well. He opened doors that eventually led me to write this book.

Other mentors appeared, sometimes at the most unexpected times. Barrie Rodgers, a renowned village-school Head in Oxfordshire, invited me to become an Assistant Master at his new open-planned school, the Queens Dyke County Primary School in Witney. His love of children, deep wisdom about what matters, and relentless standards opened me to the challenges and rewards of progressive education. David Mallery, counselor and friend to countless educators, befriended me and encouraged me to expand my horizons. His last letter to me in response to early chapters from this book praised its perspective and compassion. Parker Palmer taught me through his writing and counsel the value of respecting our inner teacher. His wisdom has guided me as I have taken my turn to write to teachers. I met Ted Sizer in his last years and am indebted to his path breaking thinking about teaching. His ideas and passion inform much of what I've written.

Rob Fried and Kim Marshall offered advice and encouragement. Rebecca Langrall and Kevin Wolgemuth willingly read early drafts and offered suggestions and insights. Barbara Barnes listened to my thinking and offered her uncanny perspectives during our nearly fifty-year friendship. I deeply appreciate the generosity of my fellow consultants from Teachers21, who have provided valuable counsel and feedback for my keynotes, workshops, and courses over the past ten years: Pam Penna, Jen Antonucci, Lyndy Johnson, Cheryl Bromley-Jones, Jerry Goldberg, Ginny Tang, Clare Fox-Ringwall, Karen Engels, George Johnson, Patti Grenier, Jenny Tsankova, Rob Traver, Sue Freedman, Peg Mongiello and Dan Price.

Of the many administrators who valued my work with their teachers, Tony Polito believed in my work early on and offered me countless opportunities to work with administrators and teachers at Narragansett and Athol. Others who have supported my work in schools: Pat Muxie and Denise Jones of Melrose; Diane Caldwell and Pat Buker of Medford; Bob Millie of Sudbury; Cathy Knowles and the Professional Development Team at Wachusett Regional High School: Chrissy Ansell, Suzanne Breen, Jen Drew, Margaret Hayes, Tess Hickey, Susan Johnson, Linda Sasso, and Leighann Wright; Joyce Croce, Cheryl Myers, and Maryann Brady of Tyngsboro; Michelle Roche and her cadre of teachers at Blue Hills Regional Tech; Pat Karl of Lawrence Family Development Charter School; Frances Cooper-Barry of Cambridge; Carolyn Cragin, formerly of East Bridgewater and Dighton-Rehoboth and now of Harwich; Pat Haggerty, formerly of Millbury and now in Auburn; Elaine Kirby, formerly of Peabody; and the late David LaPierre of Montachusett Vocational Tech.

I am also indebted to the countless colleagues who worked alongside me, down the hallways, and throughout the schools in which I taught. While in New Hampshire; Worcester, Massachusetts; Oxfordshire, England; Russia; and Kazakhstan, I had the privilege to know and value colleagues who taught me much about good teaching. And, I honor the many parents who challenged, provoked, and supported my efforts to teach their children well, especially when I chose to try innovative ideas.

I am especially indebted to Peabody High School's ninth grade teachers, who in October 2006 allowed me to observe in their classrooms and stimulated me to write this book.

I cannot remember a time when I did not write. For years, I wrote countless one-page-provocations inviting my students to consider new ways of thinking, alternative approaches to issues, and fresh strategies for analysis. Occasionally, I wrote op-ed pieces and articles for publications. Only towards the end of my classroom teaching did I consider writing to a wider audience. After several stints teaching in the former Soviet Union and Russia, I wrote some op-ed pieces and drafted a manuscript, *Through Their Eyes: Encounters with Soviet People*, which has not been published.

Besides the wonderful counsel I have received from the writing of William Strunk, Jr. and E. B. White, William Zinsser, John Trimble, Annie Dillard, and Ann Lamott, I took a writing class with Jack Shepherd that opened me to finding my own voice. His mantra "you need to be able to write your book in one sentence" has guided me ever since. John Maguire, a fellow writer and teacher of writing, offered many insights over coffee.

Finally, I must acknowledge the wise and insightful counsel of Christina Ward, my editor and my friend, who set me on the path toward publication and shepherded me through the process; Joyce Barnes for her meticulous and miraculous copyediting; and Janis Owens of Books By Design, Inc. for her expert cover design, layout and production. And a special thank you to my wife, Kathleen Cammarata, whose critiques kept me honest with myself—and with my readers.

Frank Thoms
Lowell, Massachusetts, May 2010

Endnotes

Introduction

1. Robert Evans, *The Human Side of School Change: Reform, Resistance, and the Real-Life Problems of Innovation* (San Francisco: Jossey-Bass, 1996), 132.
2. Ibid., 132–33.
3. Marc Prensky, "Digital Natives, Digital Immigrants." (2001). http://www.marcprensky.com.
4. See Ken Robinson, *Out of Our Minds: Learning to be Creative* (Chichester, West Sussex: Capstone, 2001), for an articulate appeal to provide an education suitable for the future.

Part I: What Can We Do Immediately?

5. Richard Selfe and Cynthia Selfe, "'Convince Me!' Valuing Multimodal Literacies and Composing Public Service Announcements." *Theory Into Practice*, Spring 2008, vol. 47, no. 2, 83–92, in *Marshall Memo 325*, May 19, 2008, 5.
6. John Saphier and Robert Gower, *The Skillful Teacher: Building Your Teaching Skills*. 5th Edition. (Carlisle, MA: Research for Better Teaching, Inc., 1997), 219.
7. Dylan Wiliam (2007), quoted by Kim Marshall at a Teachers21 Retreat, "Insights from Research and Practice," June 11, 2008.
8. John Saphier and Robert Gower, *The Skillful Teacher*, 309.
9. This latter application of wait time came from Laura Reasoner Jones in *Teacher Magazine*, September 3, 2008.
10. Margaret Wheatley, *Turning to One Another: Simple Conversations to Restore Hope to the Future* (San Francisco: Berret-Koehler, 2002), 29.
11. See also "A Glossary of Banned Words, Usages, Stereotypes, and Topics" (thirty-five pages!), in Appendix 1 in Diane Ravitch, *The Language Police: How Pressure Groups Restrict What Students Learn* (New York: Vintage, 2003, 2004).
12. See Chapter 1, "Implement 10-2 Thinking," p. 5 for a description of 21st century skills.
13. See *Marshall Memo 307* (October 26, 2009), summary of "Getting It Wrong: Surprising Tips on How to Learn" by Henry Roediger and Bridgid Finn in *Scientific American*, October 20, 2009; appeared in *ASCD SmartBrief*, October 21, 2009.
14. Delmar W. Goodwin, "A Manual for the Writing of Research Papers." Hanover Junior-Senior High School, Hanover, New Hampshire, 1964.

15. See Chapter 26, "Begin at the End," pp. 193–195 for a description of the backwards design process.
16. Michael Schmoker, *Results Now: How We Can Achieve Unprecedented Improvement in Teaching and Learning* (Alexandria, VA: ASCD, 2006), for literacy; and, Tony Wagner, *The Global Achievement Gap* (New York: Basic Books, 2008), for 21st century skills.
17. Thanks to Chuck Emery of Powder Mill Middle School for suggesting to use primary-color markers.
18. Peter Weir, *Dead Poets Society*, Touchstone Pictures, 1989.
19. Arthur Koestler, *The Act of Creation* (London: Hutchinson, 1964), 183–84. Koestler refers to the June 1961 issue of *Scientific American* as his source, but he remarks that the problem originates with the psychologist Carl Duncker.
20. Susan Saulny, "They Stand When Called Upon, and When Not," the *New York Times*, February 25, 2009 (A1, 15), available at http://www.nytimes.com, in *Marshall Memo 275*, March 2, 2009.
21. John Quinn, Brian Kavanagh, Norma Boakes, and Ronald Caro, "Two Thumbs Way, Way Up: Index Card Recap and Review." *Teaching Children Mathematics*, December 2008/January 2009. The National Council of Teachers of Mathematics, 295–303. With thanks to Ginny Tang who led me to this source.
22. Ibid., 300, adapted.
23. Ibid., 297, adapted.
24. Ibid., 303. The authors claim Recap Cards to be one of the more innovative approaches, alongside implementing NCTM standards. The results were impressive: One hundred percent of the students in the class described in the article passed New Jersey's fourth-grade mathematics assessment with seventy-three percent advanced proficient.
25. From Jon Saphier and Mary Ann Haley, *Summarizers: Activity Structures to Support Integration and Retention of New Learning* (Carlisle, MA: Research for Better Teaching, 1993). Along with *Activators: Activity Structures to Engage Student's Thinking Before Instruction* (Research for Better Teaching, 1993), are invaluable reproducible resources for mobilizing learning at both ends of a lesson.
26. Ibid.
27. Ibid.
28. See Ross Greene, *The Explosive Child* (New York: Harper, 2001), 287–91.
29. With thanks to Barbara Delaney, Bellingham Middle School, Massachusetts, who found these questions at a Drexel Math workshop.

Part II: How Can We Develop Our Teaching Practice?

30. Richard Lavoie, "It's So Much Work Being Your Friend: Helping the Child with Learning Disabilities Find Social Success." Speech at Fitchburg State, March 9, 2009.
31. Daniel H. Pink, *A Whole New Mind: Why Right Brainers Will Rule the Future* (New York: Penguin, 2005, 2006), 57–59.
32. Jonah Lehrer, "Don't: The Secret of Self-control." *The New Yorker,* May 18, 2009.
33. The Efficacy Institute, Inc., http://www.efficacy.org/.
34. Jon Saphier and Robert Gower, *The Skillful Teacher*, 319–20.
35. Ibid., 334.
36. Ibid., 296.
37. See Chapter 12, "Abolish Tracking," for a deeper discussion on this issue.
38. Louis Untermeyer, *New England Anthology of Robert Frost's Poems* (New York: Washington Square Press, 1971), 223.
39. Shunryu Suzuki, *Zen Mind, Beginner's Mind* (New York: Weatherhill, 1970), 21.
40. Thich Nhat Hanh, *The Miracle of Mindfulness* (Boston: Beacon Press, 1975), 4.
41. Ibid., 4, adapted.
42. Rainer Maria Rilke, *Letters to a Young Poet*, trans. Stephen Mitchell. Letter #4. http://www.sfgoth.com/~immanis/rilke/index.html.
43. Stephen Mitchell, trans. *Tao Te Ching* (New York: Harper Collins, 1988), 36.
44. Ibid., 67.
45. Adapted from Scott Peck, *The Different Drum* (New York: Simon and Shuster, 1987), 13–15. Also the full story can be found at http://www.community4me.com/rabbisgift.html, with a link to shortened version.
46. Stephen Mitchell, trans. *Tao Te Ching*, 11.
47. Hafiz, *The Gift*, trans. Daniel Ladinsky (Penguin Compass, 1999), 87.
48. Frederick Wiseman, *Meat* (documentary), 1976.
49. Jonathan Haidt. *The Happiness Hypothesis: Finding Modern Truth in Ancient Wisdom* (New York: Basic Books, 2006).
50. See text of the monk on the mountain problem in Chapter 5, "Rearrange Rooms," p. 31.
51. Google was first incorporated as a privately held company, September 4, 1998.
52. From a conversation with Bud Brooks, July 29, 2009.
53. David Sousa, *How the Brain Learns: A Classroom Teacher's Guide.* Revised Edition. (Thousand Oaks, CA: Corwin Press, 2001), 90.
54. See *Marshall Memo*, http://www.marshallmemo.com.

55. See *The Main Idea*, http://themainidea.net/index.htm.
56. Richard Dufour, et al., *Learning by Doing* (Bloomington, IN: Solution Tree, 2006); Heidi Hayes Jacobs, *Active Literacy Across the Curriculum* (Larchmont, NY: Eye on Education, 2006); Richard Stiggins, et al., *Classroom Assessment for Student Learning* (Princeton, NJ: Educational Testing Service, 2007); John Saphier, et al., *The Skillful Teacher* (Carlisle, MA: Research for Better Teaching, Inc., 2008), in two parts; and Ross Greene's, *Lost at School: Why Our Kids with Behavioral Challenges are Falling Through the Cracks and How We Can Help Them* (New York: Scribner, 2008).
57. Harry K. and Rosemary T. Wong, *The First Days of School* (Harry K. Wong Publications, Inc., 2004).
58. This metaphor is explored by Malcolm Gladwell, "How David Beats Goliath," *The New Yorker*, May 11, 2009, 40–49.
59. See the Appendix, "A Teaching Manifesto."

Part III: What Must We Change?

60. *Differentiating Instruction: Creating Multiple Paths for Learning I*, "Differentiating Activities" (ASCD, 1997).
61. *Differentiating Instruction: Creating Multiple Paths for Learning I*, "Differentiating Content" (ASCD, 1997).
62. *Differentiating Instruction: Creating Multiple Paths for Learning I*, "Differentiating Content and Activities" (ASCD, 1997).
63. Daniel H. Pink, *Whole New Mind*, 57–59.
64. Jonah Lehrer, "Don't: The Secret of Self-control," 32.
65. American Playhouse Theatrical, *Stand and Deliver*, 1998.
66. Carol Dweck, *Mindset: The New Psychology of Success* (New York: Ballantine, 2006), 194–95.
67. Mel Stuart, *The Hobart Shakespeareans*, (Docudrama.com, 2006).
68. American Playhouse Theatrical, *Stand and Deliver*.
69. Zay Smith, Chicago Sun-Times, quoting from *Marva Collins and Civia Tamarkin, Marva Collins' Way: Returning to Excellence in Education* (Los Angeles: Jeremy Tarcher, 1982/1990), 47, in Carol Dweck, *Mindset*, 199.
70. Mel Stuart, *Hobart Shakespeareans*.
71. Marianne Williamson, *A Return to Love* (Harper Collins, 1992), Chapter 7, Section 3.
72. Carol S. Dweck, *Mindset*. Thanks to Mary Anton-Oldenberg for bringing this book to my attention.
73. See for example, John Sutton and Alice Krueger, eds. *EDThoughts: What We Know About Mathematics Teaching and Learning* (Aurora, CO: McREL: Mid-continent Research for Education and Learning, 2002). (220), 4–5.

74. Richard Lavoie, "It's So Much Work Being Your Friend." He also says inclusion students do not always benefit.

75. Jerome Bruner, *The Process of Education: A Searching Discussion of School Education Opening New Paths to Learning and Teaching* (New York: Vintage, 1960), 33.

76. Tom Vreeland, Mount Everett High School, Sheffield, Massachusetts.

77. Malcolm Gladwell. *Blink: The Power of Thinking Without Thinking* (New York: Little Brown. 2005), 88–96.

78. See Chapter 6, "Make Meaning," in the section "TAPS Template for Teacher Planning" for more about how to use these questions to design lessons.

79. Stephen Herek, *Mr. Holland's Opus*, 1995.

80. It would be unfair not to acknowledge instances of union leadership that exert a positive influence on improving education. Brian Gearty of Blue Hills Regional Vocational School in Canton, Massachusetts, and Robert Becker of Wachusett Regional School District in Holden, Massachusetts, are examples of two leaders I have met. Unfortunately, such people are too rare.

81. Michael Schmoker, *Results Now*, 37, cites David Berliner's reports of the chaos in curriculum.

82. Michael Jones, "Grade the Teachers: A Way to Improve Schools on Instructor at a Time." *Boston Globe*, November 1, 2009.

83. Marilyn Marks, "The Teacher Factor." *The New York Times*, Education Life Supplement. January 9, 2000.

84. William Damon, *Greater Expectations: Overcoming the Culture of Indulgence in Our Homes and Schools* (New York: Free Press, 1996), 32.

85. Ibid., 200.

86. Robert Evans, (2001), "National Seminar for the Experienced Pro," Mallery Seminars, Philadelphia, Pennsylvania.

87. Steven Pressfield, *The War of Art* (New York: Warner Books, 2002), 20–21.

88. Coleen Armstrong, "Do Not Disturb!" *Teacher Magazine*, May/June 1995.

89. Patti Grenier, now Superintendent of the Barnstable Public Schools, Massachusetts, shared this research at a workshop in Pittsfield, Massachusetts, January 2004.

90. James W. Stigler and James Hiebert, *The Teaching Gap: Best Ideas from the World's Teachers for Improving Education in the Classroom* (New York: Free Press, 1999), 55–56.

91. Lorraine K. Hong, "Too Many Intrusions on Instructional Time." *Phi Delta Kappan*, May 2001, 712–14.

92. Ibid., 714.

93. "Will the BlackBerry Sink the Presidency?" by Sharon Begley in *Newsweek*, February 16, 2009, 37, excerpted in the *Marshall Memo* 274, February 23, 2009.

94. For example, Peabody High School and Wachusett Regional High School in Massachusetts, both with nearly 2000 students, do not allow the PA to be used during the day.

95. Tim Healey, "Creating Greatness." *Principal Leadership*, February 2009, 31, in *Marshall Memo* 272, February 9, 2009, 1.

96. Carol Ann Tomlinson, "Mapping a Route Towards Instruction." *Educational Leadership*, vol. 57, no. 1, 1999, 12–16.

97. J. D. Bransford, A. L. Brown, and R. R. Cocking, eds., *How People Learn: Brain, Mind, Experience, and School*. Expanded edition. (Committee on Developments in the Science of Learning, National Research Council, National Academy Press, 2000), 20.

98. With thanks from Debra Spinelli who shared this anonymous quotation with me.

99. See Figure 6.1. The TAPS Template for Teacher Planning, in Chapter 6, "Make Meaning," for a graphic representation of Ms. Cassell's approach.

100. See Chapter 12, "Abandon the Crabs in the Cage."

101. See Chapter 1, "Implement 10-2 Thinking," for a detailed discussion.

102. Robert Sternberg, in Carol Dweck, *Mindset*, 5.

103. See Figure 6.2, Give One/Get One as Review, in Chapter 6, "Make Meaning."

104. Teachers often tell me that such lessons are fine for history and English, but not for mathematics or science. I beg to differ, as these disciplines raise many questions. For example, math students could wrestle with inventing solutions to open-ended problems and defend their solutions to their classmates rather than sit and listen to the teacher instruct day after day.

105. See Exit Cards, in Chapter 6, "Make Meaning," pp. 37–38.

106. See Figure 6.3. TAPS Template for Teacher Planning, Chapter 6, "Make Meaning."

Part IV: What Can We Learn from Beyond the Culture of Schools?

107. Malcolm Gladwell, *The Tipping Point: How Little Things Can Make A Big Difference* (New York: Little, Brown and Company, 2002).

108. This concept is explored in Chapter 12, "Abandon the Crabs in the Cage."

109. Stephen C. Lundin, Harry Paul, and John Christianson, *Fish! A Remarkable Way to Boost Morale and Improve Results* (New York: Hyperion, 2000).

110. Paul Hawken, on *The Paula Gordon Show*, January 15, 2010, at http://www.paulagordon.com/content/suicide-interventions.

111. The rider and elephant metaphor is explained in Chapter 9, "Stay Current."

112. Chip Heath and Dan Heath, *Made to Stick: Why Some Ideas Survive and Others Die* (Random House, 2007, 2008). An essential for teachers!

113. Ibid. This summary was adapted from material on the authors' Website, which offers free materials specifically for teachers. http://www.madetostick.com.

114. Martha Graham to Agnes de Mille, *Dance to the Piper* (New York: De Capo Press, 1980), 335–36, in Paul Hawken, *Blessed Unrest How the Largest Movement in the World Came into Being and Why No One Saw It Coming* (New York: Penguin Group, 2007), 9.

115. See Chapter 12, "Abandon the Crabs in the Cage," p. 102 for an explanation of the Golden Toilet award.

116. Laura Miller, "Far From Narnia: Philip Pullman's Secular Fantasy for Children." *The New Yorker.* December 26, 2005 & January 1, 2006, 3.

117. Ibid.

118. "Elliot Eisner on the Deep Stuff That Schools Should Teach," in *Marshall Memo* 17, December 15, 2003, 3–4. http://marshallmemo.com.

119. For a list of Marzano's ten questions, Jan Umphrey, "Producing Learning: A Conversation with Robert Marzano," in *Principal Leadership*, January 2008, vol. 8, no. 5, 16–20, in Marshall Memo 217, January 15, 2008, 2–3.

120. Ross Greene, *Lost at School: Why Our Kids with Behavioral Challenges are Falling Through the Cracks and How We Can Help Them* (New York: Scribner, 2008).

121. Brian Swimme, at the Institute of Religion in the Age of Science Conference, Star Island, Portsmouth, New Hampshire, August 2005. His seminal work with Thomas Berry, *The Universe Story: From the Primordial Flaring Forth to the Ecozoic Era—A Celebration of the Unfolding of the Cosmos* (Harper Collins, 1992), has brought forth the new creation story based on recent cosmological research.

122. This idea comes from the thoughtfulness of Stacey Ake in a personal communication.

123. Susanne Rubenstein, Wachusett High School, *Teacher Magazine*, August/September, 1999, excerpted in the journal *ClassWise*, October, 1999.

124. Ken Wilber, *A Brief History of Everything* (Boston: Shambhala, 1996), 20.

125. Ibid., 20–22.

126. Stacey Ake, Assistant Professor of Philosophy in the English and Philosophy Department at Drexel University, in a personal communication.

127. Fred Jervis, Founder and President of the Center for Constructive Change, Durham, New Hampshire, speaking in Hanover, New Hampshire, August 1982.

Part V: How Do We Find Our Calling?

128. James Hillman, *The Soul's Code: In Search of Character and Calling* (New York: Warner Books, 1997), 6.

129. Example from Matthew Adiletta, Intel Fellow and Director of Communication Infrastructure and Architecture in the Intel Architecture Group, speaking at Clark University, March 26, 2001.

130. John Updike, from his 1990 *Boston Globe* interview, reported in the *Boston Globe*, January 28, 2009.

131. Michael Schmoker, *Results Now*, 4–5.

132. Robert Marzano, from Kim Marshall, "Insights from Research and Practice."

133. Christopher Boone, Head of the Middle School at Bancroft School, Worcester, Massachusetts, 1996–2001, brought a progressive and caring understanding of middle school teaching and learning to a mixed-age staff. His untimely death at 34 years old was a terrible loss.

134. Randy Pausch, "Last Lecture : Achieving Your Childhood Dreams," http://www.youtube.com/watch?v=ji5_MqicxSo—A worthwhile one hour and a half! See also Randy Pausch and Jeffrey Zaslow. *The Last Lecture* (New York: Hyperion, 2008).

135. Parker Palmer, *The Courage to Teach: Exploring the Inner Landscape of a Teacher's Life* (San Francisco: Jossey-Bass, 1998), Introduction, 1. Still the most profound book on reflecting on the meaning of teaching.

136. Michael Schmoker, *Results Now*, "Introduction: The Brutal Facts About Instruction and Supervision," 1–10.

137. See National Board for Professional Teaching Standards, http://www.nbpts.org.

138. Harry K. Wong and Rosemary T. Wong, *The First Days of School: How To Be An Effective Teacher* (Mountainview, CA: Harry K. Wong Productions, Inc., 1998), 6.

139. See the video, "Ken Robinson Says Schools Kill Creativity," TED2006, February 2006, http://www.ted.com/talks/ken_robinson_says_schools_kill_creativity.html.

140. Steve Almond, "Blogged to Death," *Boston Globe*, Op-ed, September 19, 2007.

141. See Nicholas Carr, "Is Google Making Us Stupid?" *The Atlantic*, July/August, 2008.

142. Justine Ezarik, a Web designer and video blogger in Pittsburgh, interview: "iPhone: A Compact Device with a Very Bulky Bill." *All Things Considered*, NPR, August 16, 2007.

143. See the videos, "Did You Know? 2.0," http://www.teachertube.com/viewVideo.php?video_id=3051&title=Did_You_Know__2_0; and "Did You Know? 3.0," http://www.teachertube.com/viewVideo.php?video_id=115106&title=Did_you_know_version_3_0.

144. "Ken Robinson Says Schools Kill Creativity," http://www.ted.com/index.php/talks/ken_robinson_says_schools_kill_creativity.html.

145. Tony Wagner, *The Global Achievement Gap*, 41.

146. Marc Prensky, "Digital Natives, Digital Immigrants."

147. Neil Swidey, "Why an iPhone could actually be good for your 3-year old." *Boston Globe*, November 1, 2009, http://www.boston.com/bostonglobe/magazine/articles/2009/11/01/why_an_iphone_could_actually_be_good_for_your_3_year_old/.

148. I derived this idea of "being pulled" from Rumi, "The Universe is for Satisfying Needs," in *The Rumi Collection*, ed. Kabir Helminski (Boston: Shambhala, 1998), 66.

149. See Chapter 8, "Search for Wisdom," p. 59 for further discussion of Robert Frost, "The Road Not Taken."

150. Grant Wiggins and Jay McTighe, *Understanding by Design* (Alexandria, VA: ASCD, 1998).

151. Robert Fried, *The Passionate Teacher: A Practical Guide* (Boston: Beacon Press, 1995), 232–33.

152. Thanks to Jen Antonucci who found this story by an unknown author on the Internet.

153. The ideas in this section have been inspired by "The Stockdale Paradox," developed by Admiral Jim Stockdale during his years in prison in Vietnam, as described by Jim Collins in *Good to Great: Why Some Companies Make the Leap . . . and Others Don't* (New York: Harper Collins, 2001), 83–87; in particular: "Retain faith that you will prevail in the end, regardless of the difficulties and at the same time confront the most brutal facts of your current reality whatever they might be," 86.

Index

Frank Thoms is a lifelong classroom teacher, consultant, and writer. He devotes himself to improving the teaching profession, one teacher at a time, to meet the challenge of today's digitally-wired, techno-literate students. He advocates that teachers become change-makers. He believes invitations offer the most powerful impetus to affect change, in stark contrast to federal, state, and local mandates that often cause resentment and resistance.

Frank has taught in public and private schools in the United States, as well as in schools in England, Russia, and Kazakhstan. He was a founding member of the exemplary Upper Valley Educators Institute, one of the nation's first alternative teacher certification programs, now in its fifth decade. He developed a model open-education classroom that served as a resource to New England schools. He has consulted for PBS, AFS Intercultural Programs, the Kettering Foundation, Association of Independent Schools of New England (AISNE), and the Vermont State Department of Education.

During the past ten years, he has served in more than one hundred twenty-five schools providing keynotes, workshops, pedagogical courses, mentoring, and teacher coaching. His unique style blends serious content and processes with an interactive format that serves as a model for the teaching he advocates throughout this book.

Frank invites readers—teachers, administrators, and concerned citizens—to contact him at his Website, http://www.stetsonpress.com, or join him at his blog, http://teachfromthemiddle.blogspot.com/. He welcomes consulting in schools as a writer/educator-in-residence, as a seminar provider, or as a keynote speaker.

Breinigsville, PA USA
11 May 2010
237791BV00004B/1/P